DISCOVER GRAPHOLOGY

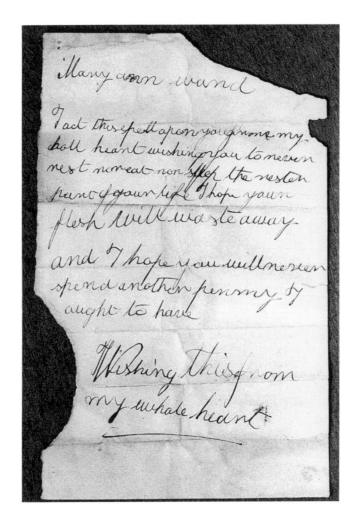

This curse, found with its curse doll within a house wall, reflects its writer's state of mind in every movement and stroke of the pen. It states:

'Mary Ann Ward
I act this spell upon you from my [w]holl heart wishing you never to rest nor eat nor sleep the rest part of your life I hope your flesh will waste away and I hope you will never spend another penny I ought to have'
Wishing this from my whole heart

(Photo courtesy of Hereford City Museums)

DISCOVER
GRAPHOLOGY

A straightforward and practical guide to handwriting analysis

MARGARET GULLAN-WHUR

Sterling Publishing Co., Inc.   New York

Library of Congress Cataloging-in-Publication Data

Gullan-Whur, Margaret.
   [Graphology workbook]
   Discover graphology : a straightforward & practical guide to
handwriting analysis / Margaret Gullan-Whur.
     p.   cm.
   Originally published: The graphology workbook. Wellingborough,
Northamptonshire : Aquarian Press ; New York, N.Y. : Distributed by
Sterling Pub. Co., 1986.
   Includes bibliographical references.
   ISBN 0-8069-0356-2
   1. Graphology.   I. Title.
   [BF891.G84   1993]
   155.9—dc20   92–44046
                                              CIP

Library of Congress Cataloging-in-Publication Data Available

1   3   5   7   9   10   8   6   4   2

Published 1993 by Sterling Publishing Company, Inc.
387 Park Avenue South, New York, N.Y. 10016
Originally published in Great Britain by
The Aquarian Press under the title *The Graphology Workbook*
© 1986, 1991 by Margaret Gullan-Whur
Distributed in Canada by Sterling Publishing
% Canadian Manda Group, P.O. Box 920, Station U
Toronto, Ontario, Canada M8Z 5P9
Manufactured in the United States of America
All rights reserved

Sterling ISBN 0-8069-0356-2

Contents

Preface

The 1980s were an important decade for British graphology. In 1983 the Graphology Society was formed, and in 1984 the British Institute of Graphology set about drawing together hitherto unlinked schools and methods of handwriting analysis, its aim being to introduce a single, unified approach to the subject. Its ultimate aim was, and is, to present an approved, official teaching syllabus for graphology students, preparing the way for academic recognition in this country. Every subject now studied in our universities had, at one time or another, to fight in this way for its eventual status, and its struggle for academic laurels was not likely to be won by rivalry and dispute amongst its myriad exponents, but through unified insistence on certain common priorities.

And so I have avoided controversial or borderline issues in this book and tried instead to present some of the accumulated learning of respected graphological tradition. This book sets out to present in a business-like way — as its title suggests — the fundamental eye-training skills needed in graphology. And although it will soon be seen that our true subject is not marks on paper, but people and their infinitely complex patterns of behaviour, we shall, in this visually accented study, be concentrating chiefly on the careful observation of some undisputed graphological findings.

The Premiss of Graphology

One flick through this book demonstrates the extraordinary variety of handwriting regularly committed to paper. Neither fashion nor teaching methods can account — nor ever could — for the diversity of pattern used to imprint the written word in regular inky traces. What, then, can?

Handwriting is an electrical impulse originating in the brain. The hand and the pen are its tools, and the inky traces — ignoring any sense in their messages — more or less resemble the angular markings of an electroencephalograph. Neuro-Linguistic Programming tests in America have shown that the fingertips can transmit brain sensations, making interpretable marks in response to questioning. Based on the 'lie detector' belief that the body reflects with immense sensitivity the psychological forces at work in the mind, Dr Robert Dilts' machine may ultimately prove correct the claims made during centuries of graphological observation.

These claims are that certain patterns and signs in the writing may be taken to indicate definite psychological traits. The Roman historian Suetonius always noted the particular characteristics of the handwriting of the emperor whose biography he was writing, and a popular but vague acceptance of some kind of link between character and handwriting is found in literary writings, but the first systematic account of such claims was published in Capri in 1622 by a medical doctor and professor of philosophy, Camillo Baldo. Studies and treatises appeared subsequently in Italy, Switzerland and France, but the subject was not likely to have intellectual appeal during the following centuries of reason and proof-based emphasis, and it remained an obscure study, not even acquiring a name.

Modern graphology originated in a circle of the higher French clergy of the mid-nineteenth century — a fact which may account for the severity of judgement still to be found in some French graphology. Credit is given to Jean Hippolyte Michon (L'Abbé Michon), a pupil of the group, who established the name graphology (grapho — I write; logos — theory or doctrine), and recorded his experienced observations in three books, published between 1870 and 1875. L'Abbé Michon produced a comprehensive catalogue of signs and rules, but he did not attempt to explain why these might hold true, nor in those days preceding the dawn of psychology as a study separate from medicine, did he try to interpret the movements in terms of mental behaviour patterns. Later European schools of graphology rejected Michon's catalogue of definite signs in favour of more subtle groupings and tendencies — patterns and trends in the writing — but we are still in Michon's debt for the proviso which accompanied each of his character assessments: it is one which present-day graphologists, especially when pressed for a snap analysis, might protect themselves and their clients by voicing: '*If* this writing is truly that of the writer, *not* disguised, but spontaneous and habitual *that is, his usual writing*), it tells us that ...' [My italics].

Michon's big IF makes the first of the pitfalls awaiting the inexperienced graphologist, and still a threat to the experienced. However truly the signs and patterns seem to be there in the writing, checking and questioning must be a part of the run-up to any analysis. Samples written specially for analysis cannot be entirely spontaneous: the electrical impulse is steadied at source. Nor do we always write in exactly the same way, depending on our inner motivation or the sensitivity of our natures to different stimuli. We need as many handwriting samples as possible, and we need to ask questions about the conditions under which they were written.

Michon's pupil Jules Crépieux-Jamin extended the noting of clearly visible signs in the writing into a more elaborate system of co-ordination of dominant signs — 175 aspects divided into seven groupings. Crépieux-Jamin lived until 1940 and was a powerful influence in European graphology. His insistence that any one sign in the writing must, like a jigsaw piece, be considered in relation to all the other signs, remains an important principle of graphology.

Whilst the French school continued with such detailed observation, the newly emerging psychological movements in Germany began to urge other graphologists to consider more deeply the psychic forces operating behind the pen. At the turn of the century, Georg Meyer and William Preyer included, with their attention to the psychoanalytic work of Freud, the importance of the biological constitution in assessing writing, thus connecting graphology with the other achievements of modern science and adding to our provisos the need to note the individual's state of health.

Ludwig Klages' *Handwriting and Character* was first published in 1917, and subsequently overshadowed all but the French tradition in graphology. The first to view handwriting in its entirety — as a picture — as the whole expression of an individual nature, he gave graphology two important methods of assessment: the general Form Level (formniveau) and the rhythm of the writing. Both depended not on signs or formations, but on the form of the writing taken as a whole, and, together with other assessments which we shall learn to recognize, they have been described by a later graphologist as the 'invisible' signs.

Robert Saudek, a Czech, wrote in English and studied English handwriting. To Klages' assessments he added the important factor of speed in writing, and to many British graphologists he is the founder of their tradition.

We owe much to a Swiss graphologist, Max Pulver, for his investigation in the first half of this century into space symbolism in writing. Interested in the psychology of the unconscious, he saw the clean white page as world space, to be filled by entering it according to one's nature, be it quickly but hesitantly, slowly and with eyes constantly turning backward to the past, or in an eager, all-embracing rush. He noted the upward reaching of the spiritually inclined, and the downward plunging strokes made by earthy natures. But he was also aware that many of these impulses are unconscious, that we are governed as much — or more — by those thoughts and feelings which never surface, as by our conscious attitudes and decisions.

The graphologist H. J. Jacoby, who came to Britain from central Europe in the 1930s, saw these movements as inherent in all nature, and he used photographs and images to draw comparisons between bodily and other natural movements within our world space. Handwriting is above all visual, and such symbolism helps to link eye-training with mental concepts.

French graphology now includes German, Swiss, Belgian, Dutch and Hungarian theories, and in the second half of the twentieth century has brought the psychology of C. G. Jung, including his *Psychological Types*, to bear upon character assessment. Ania Teillard, French graphologist and a student of Jung, was the first to write a graphology book in which an understanding of depth psychology was placed before all else — before, indeed considering embarking upon the analysis of handwriting. It is likely that psychology will be included in the forthcoming British syllabus, and we should remember that the studies of psychology and graphology each have a documented history of little more than a hundred years, and must advance hand in hand. We should also remember that man's understanding of himself in past civilizations was of humbling depth and scope, and we should draw on that wisdom, too.

In America at least thirty-two different societies exist to teach or promote graphology, some using methods which are not easily combined with other systems. At present there are no plans for unifying them all, but each has something to contribute to the study.

Graphologists who have worked for up to fifty years in near isolation with no supporting organization and only books or perhaps a private tutor to help them, are the true founders of British graphology. They have done much to widen the field of its application and to attract public confidence. John Beck, Frank Hilliger and Patricia Marne, the founders of our Society and our Institute, should be mentioned in particular. Professionally qualified people who have been brave enough to support this hitherto fringe or alternative aid to human understanding, and who speak out for its reliability as an indicator of the individual's current psychological state, are furthering its development as greatly as have the pioneers above. Let us be grateful to them all, and consider before we set to work their gifts of courage and caution, meticulous observation and willingness to absorb new ideas about man's nature.

This book, setting out as it does to be eclectic rather than personal, takes a different approach to graphology from *What Your Handwriting Reveals*, my earlier book. That was the result of nearly thirty years' lonely study and research, and it still has a great deal to add to the contents of this book of basics. Here, we are establishing an *agreed general principle* for each trait, with discussion on how to recognize it. The general principle is printed in italics, and the trait it describes is in **bold** type.

There is no particular virtue in the ordering of the material, but the arrangement has a logic of its own, as is suggested by the section headings. Each trait has to be learned in principle, and the charts on pages 157 and 158 show all those universally shared, while omitting some of the finer points of Continental and American graphology, many of which are subject to disagreement. It is time enough to move into those areas when the basics are clear. There is no index because understanding in depth depends on the consideration of all graphological aspects, each of which appears in the Contents list and as a heading.

Throughout, we must try to look over and above the carefully learned pieces of the jigsaw at the whole, unique picture of the writing of each individual. The book begins and ends with this holistic (wholistic) approach, and those who would give graphology — which is by nature both science and art — the additional status of a caring 'profession', will rid themselves now of any gossip instinct or impulse to make moral judgements on others, and gird themselves instead with caution, compassion and tact.

Introduction to the New Edition: Graphology — The State of the Art as We Discover It

Most people living in developed countries today will have heard of graphology. Unfortunately much misinformation is disseminated, and media coverage is often given to the sensational and speculative. It is not surprising therefore that those unaware of the highly disciplined practice of legitimate graphology consider handwriting analysis to be slightly disreputable, and that others who are drawn to the subject want to know more about its credentials. They wonder how they are going to explain their new interest to friends, or how they can justify employing a graphologist. All these people deserve more information.

Graphology as a Science

Disciplines seeking public approval strive for academic recognition. University departments will close their doors against any practice which fails to meet certain rational or empirical criteria. Such criteria are culturally decided: they don't represent universal or eternal truths. Until the seventeenth century all European physicians were required to demonstrate an extensive understanding of astrology; until well into the twentieth century scholars needed to know Latin.

There may never have been a culture in which the requirement to demonstrate academic expertise was more stringent than our own. Tokens and symbols of credibility and paper qualifications are the expected norm. What is demanded far more than practical ability is proof of methodological understanding; this attitude permeates all current academic and technical disciplines. The reason is this: we live in an age in which empirical science predominates overwhelmingly. This is evident in many social practices. Television commercials give causal explanations for their product's success: we change our eating habits at the drop of a media headline. Where activities of the human body are concerned we generally take science as our guide.

I have until recently followed the Chinese tradition, which does not distinguish between arts and sciences, recognizing instead relevant informative material in whatever guise it appears. But questions which are frequently asked express a social need, and I am asked increasingly about the nature of graphology — science or art? It is no longer satisfactory to answer that graphology is both an art and a science. Many people want to understand what constitutes a science, and to know whether the practice of graphology is scientific or not. I hope what follows will help frame answers to these questions.

It is difficult to deny that handwriting is an activity of the human body, or that the claims of graphology come within the scope of scientific enquiry. Graphology claims that specific handwriting movements indicate specific character traits. This invites comparison with diagnostic medicine, where it might be claimed that particular pink spots on the skin indicate physical condition x or y; or with animal behavioural psychology, where it is claimed, for example, that the rhesus monkey's simple stare signifies hostility. It is admitted by at least one behavioural psychologist that handwriting is an attractive expressive field.[1] But the claims of medicine and behavioural psychology are based on adequate research; they are not hypotheses offered without substantial and rigorous testing.

To establish itself as a science a study must codify its basic assumptions, set them forth plainly and allow them to be verified. The philosopher of science Karl Popper sums it up neatly: 'The criterion of the scientific status of a theory is its falsifiability, or refutability, or testability.'[2] Popper adds that this criterion solves any problem of marking off scientific from non-scientific discourse, since statements or systems of statements, in order to be ranked as scientific, must be capable of conflicting with observation. Testing is empirical, that is, decided by observation and experience. Speculation and guesswork are allowed in the construction of the hypothesis or initial claim, but they have no place in scientific conclusions. Generally described as 'confirmed' 'upheld' or 'corroborated' (or falsified!) these conclusions are the result of observations carried out by adequate observers — people capable of conducting a test according to scientific standards. They must be given clearly defined variables — in this case particular handwriting traits and specific character modes. These must be of non-perspectival material, meaning that all definitions are stated in terms understood by any competent user of the language.

The conditions outlined above confer minimal scientific status. Science doesn't require causal mechanisms to be demonstrated. All that it requires at this stage is that a correlation be properly established between the handwriting trait or traits (a limited and clearly defined group) and the character trait or state of affairs it is claimed to signify. Science demands that when we say that a specific writing trait or traits indicates specific character traits we are also saying that this has been attested. In time the whole system of psycho-physical causal connections might be testable. Graphology is well placed to claim a complete system of causal connections, since brain states, which it is believed cause particular character traits, are known to be responsible for handwriting.

We have to distinguish between signs of physical functional disturbance or disease as shown in the handwriting, and signs indicating character traits or states of affairs which are psychological, not physical, phenomena. The former may be closely observed and monitored. Orthodox medicine relies on writing patterns to indicate particular physical conditions, and work on this is being extended. An example is M. Wilson's *Case Study of a Brain Tumour*, which investigates past writing samples of a patient suffering from both epilepsy and a fatal brain tumour.[3] Signs of the brain tumour and of the onset of epileptic convulsions were found in samples written long before any clinical evidence appeared. The handwriting evidence was found to date back to the patient at the age of eleven, one year after he suffered a mild head injury. Sadly he died aged thirty-three.

The scientific validation of the correlation of handwriting traits with functional disturbance or particular states of disease involves measurable and generally clearly observable processes, and is therefore less contentious than the validation of graphology's central claim: that specific movements in the handwriting indicate specific character traits. Nor can the corroboration of the former validate the latter claim. The character states or traits that graphologists claim to recognize must inevitably arise from extremely subtle and complex brain states, as the rest of this book illustrates. Further, many of those character traits are not overt. They may be unconscious as far as the writer is concerned, though they must be recognizable by at least one of an observer's senses for them to be tested and verified. It is this aspect of graphology that concerns practising graphologists, as well as any members of the general public whom their practice is likely to affect.

Since 1983 responsible graphological organizations have forbidden their members to diagnose disease or disturbed functional states from movements in the script, since rash or erroneous judgements may be made by those unqualified to recognize organic disorders. This stricture does not exclude high-level research in this important application of graphology, but inexperienced practitioners such as the readers of this book are unlikely to be involved in such work unless they are also medically qualified.

Our main concern is with the scientific validation of orthodox graphology; with the claim that specific writing patterns indicate specific character traits or psychological states of affairs. It is not sufficient to claim that generations of graphologists have found these correlations to be true. This is an inductive conclusion, and while this process is used in science it can appear to validate correlations that are either untestable or if tested might be falsified. Inductive corroboration is the basis of enduring old wives' tales. It is in the interest of any claim to being a matter of fact to submit itself to testing by observation and experiment, thus establishing for itself an empirical basis in fact.

Testing procedures can be applied to any theory that is derived inductively and is testable because observable. In the case of graphology this is what is happening: I will give two brief examples.

Testable correlation (1) is that the handwriting of medical doctors is less legible than that of other individuals. In this example a large number of Australian doctors and non-doctors were asked for writing samples. The samples were graded and four different statistical tests were performed on the results. In all four tests the doctors' handwriting was less legible than that of the others. Therefore the hypothesis was upheld by the *Medical Journal of Australia* (1976, 2 (12) pp. 462–3).[4] It should be noted that this test was not conducted by graphologists and that the variables were clearly stated. There was no mystery about this hypothesis or its verification. My explanation of why doctors' handwriting is illegible, given in *What Your Handwriting Reveals* (Aquarian, 1984, p. 34), could be properly tested to provide a fuller conclusion.

Testable correlation (2) is that a woman who continues to write in copybook style (see p. 36 below) is less likely to be as well-educated or intelligent as the woman who has developed a more original, efficient way of writing. The writings of 150 women were selected from files and the letters *d*, *g* and *f* were examined. Besides the copybook versions, five versions of *d*, six of *g* and six of *f* were identified, and their presence or absence was noted. Ages, educational records and intelligence quotients (Weschler scales) were correlated with handwriting. The results of the testing were affirmed by E. Epstein, H. Hartford and I. Tumarkin in *The Journal of Experimental Education* (Vol. 29 No. 4. June 1961 pp. 385–392).[5] It should be noted that the test was properly conducted, without any graphological guidance, but that the handwriting traits selected are not the only ways in which handwriting can deviate from copybook, and this might have affected the conclusions. Further, the conclusions are partially derived from correlating handwriting traits with the findings of psychometric tests, as discussed below.

Testing is time-consuming and requires knowledgeable monitoring, particularly of data analysis. It is therefore expensive. For maximum credibility it should be conducted by impartial (that is, non-graphologist) observers. The difficulty connected with this is that those who offer to conduct such tests very often construct their own hypotheses; they make claims for graphology which no well-trained graphologist would make. Or they use a bizarre speculation from an individual graphologist. There are two points to be made here, both directly connected with the methodology of empirical science.

First, graphological correlations, if they are to satisfy scientific criteria, need to be standardized. This book attempts to do that. Second, scientific practices or disciplines which deal with the general public and take money in payment are subject to the standards insisted upon by their own disciplinary bodies. It is the mark of a practice seeking official recognition that it establishes such a disciplinary body, and it is the mark of a scientifically-orientated practitioner that he or she joins and gains accreditation from such an institute. It is noticeable that graphologists who do not want academic or institutional patronage tend to avoid disciplinary bodies and refuse to apply for accreditation. This is discussed below from the viewpoint of someone seeking an artistic or intuitive status for graphology. If you are looking for a graphology teacher and you would like as scientific a graphologist as possible, ask for his or her accreditation and check up on what that accreditation is worth.

More and more scientific research is being carried out using hypothesis testing. British graphology has been re-orientated and transformed since the advent early in the 1980s of three graphological bodies: the British Institute of Graphologists, the Graphology Society, and the Academy of Graphology (addresses are listed on page 176). All three have high standards of practice and insist that no graphological judgement is made without evidence being given of specific traits and their accepted correlations. All welcome further research.

As a form of behavioural expression handwriting can be precisely measured over a long period of time, though it should be remembered that it records the brain state at a given moment in time. Basic hypotheses relating to the central claim of graphology have been tested at various institutes and universities, and by competent private groups throughout the world.[6] Many more tests are planned or are underway.

Graphology does not need to be a mystery, transcending empirical enquiry and taken on faith like a religion. It is now over thirty years since the German professor Pophal's slow-motion studies of handwriting movements in the air were carried out. He found them highly individualistic and characteristic for every person.[7] Evidence of substantiated correlations, or of encouraging exploratory studies, are to be found in many learned journals.

It has to be said that because of the cultural values and scientific bias of the times we live in, those graphologists who do not care if graphology is considered scientific or not nevertheless benefit greatly from the meticulous research carried out on behalf of their study.

Graphology as a Branch of Psychology

Graphology's central claim makes it an ethological tool, and any means of studying character belongs rightly within the discipline of psychology, either empirical or behavioural. There are very few centres of behavioural or experimental psychology, but it could be that graphology's criteria are acceptable there. Its character-trait variables would need however to be overt and observable: This would put a considerable limitation on a study that prides itself on cryptanalysis — the interpretation of hidden signs — and claims to recognize unconscious impulses in handwriting. Nevertheless, whatever could be established through such research would be, as was Pophal's work, of very great value in verifying graphology as a scientifically reliable diagnostic tool.

If graphology is taught at all in British universities, it is likely to be treated as a branch of psychology. This is by no means certain, however: courses focusing on graphology alone are already taught at British institutes of higher education.[8] The question under discussion here is how graphology might come to be included in an academic course in psychology; how it might be considered a branch of psychology.

Its success can be measured against the findings of various well-established psychological or psychometric tests, as we established in the case of the 'intelligent women' test above. Advanced education can be measured by observing academic records, but intelligence cannot. It is a very difficult variable to measure, so the researcher uses accepted scales of measurement known as intelligence quotients. Though these psychometric tests are much used it is not claimed that they are completely infallible. Since people tend to achieve higher intelligence quotients on tests conducted within their own cultural administration, it seems probable that there is a larger element of cultural agreement on what constitutes intelligence, and less objectivity, than might at first have been thought. It is my opinion that school records provide a less contentious conclusion on educational attainment than can any particular psychometric intelligence test. I believe there are many kinds of applied intelligence (for each of which the particular brain state might be found to be quite different), and many varied manifestations of it in writing.[9] Tests would be more accurate if particular types of intelligence were defined and examined — for example the ability to make logical connections.

Psychologists using their own psychometric scales require agreed, non-negotiable psychological descriptions in order to test graphology successfully. This may call for instructing graphologists in the methodology of psychology. Several papers have been published correlating graphological and psychometric findings. Psychologists concerned with the validation procedures of graphology may want to consult psychologist/graphologist Patricia Wellingham-Jones.[10] No one has carried out more individual research or worked harder to create a bibliography of European research articles.

As we have seen, graphology can be validated as a branch of psychology by the correlation of its findings with those of psychometric tests, the conclusions of which can be subsequently tested by the hypothetico-deductive method. Psychology is not (by its own admission) an exact science, but it *is* an accepted academic discipline, and its methodology meets scientific criteria as far as its subject matter allows.

Any study that investigates human behaviour deals as a matter of course with more than the purely physical matter dealt with by the natural sciences. Modern empirical psychology is far removed from its beginnings, but it is perhaps helpful to look at these historical foundations. It was the task of its first practitioners to determine the extent to which the study of the human mind could be described as a science. Jung was explicit:

> In respect of its natural subject matter and its method of procedure, modern empirical psychology belongs to the natural sciences, but in respect of its method of explanation it belongs to the humane sciences. . . . Our psychology takes account of the cultural as well as the natural man, and accordingly its explanations must keep both points of view in mind, the spiritual and the biological. . . . Our psychology is therefore an eminently practical science. It does not investigate for investigation's sake, (though I think that is not true of all modern experimental psychology) but for the immediate purpose of giving help. We could even say that learning is its by-product, but not its principal aim, which is again a great difference from what one means by 'academic science'.[11]

Jung was a particular kind of psychologist — three kinds, in fact. He was a psychiatrist, i.e., a doctor practising psychology as a branch of medicine; an analytical psychologist using the method of free analysis to draw out the contents of the unconscious mind; and a psychotherapist, one who helps the psychically disturbed to an autonomous understanding of their problem, thereby emphasizing the individual's own role in his or her recovery. Depth psychologists such as Jung, or Freud, believed that the feelings, fantasies and attitudes to the future buried in the unconscious are all part of the truth about a person's character, and could not be neatly cut off from what was overt and observable. Freud's investigations of the effects of the unconscious workings of the mind followed Darwin's establishment of man as an animal amongst other animals. Freud was sure that another vision of behavioural cause, our 'instinctual wishful impulses', was needed. He pointed out that psychology follows the 'slow, laborious and hesitating' path of science, 'but has to do without the assistance afforded to research by experiment.'[12] For psychology deals in part with an aspect of the mind not directly amenable to monitoring — the unconscious.

The psychological descriptions of behaviour variables used in modern psychology are generally carefully constructed as conceptual models which can stand for physological processes. Nevertheless, the strictures of the depth psychologists remain true: it is very difficult to be objective about character states, which are after all not overt, not admitted and only with great effort intersubjectively defined.

Freud never repented that psychoanalysis attained only minimal scientific status. Even when he was told by patients that he was wrong and hadn't solved their problems, he protested that their very denial meant that they could not recognize the truths he had discovered, and so prevented their own cure. This is certainly a problem met with by graphologists! Freud's methods were largely unscientific and his conclusions correspondingly unfalsifiable. Critics have accused him of avoiding the possibility of falsification by blaming his patients, and of redefining the words 'cure' and 'unhappiness' to suit himself.[13] But in a discussion of the characteristics and discoveries of his practice, he said he would make 'no sacrifice to an appearance of being simple, complete or rounded off', nor would he 'disguise problems nor deny the existence of gaps and uncertainties'.[14]

Thus, despite Freud's claims to accept a scientific *Weltanschauung*, or conceptual umbrella, he effectively abandoned it. Graphologists who correlate their findings with his definitions should remember this. His 'complexes' may be little different to the psychological types of Jung — virtually untestable, but akin to the closed systems of metaphor discussed below. Science is precise. It simplifies and insists on definitions (which may be cruder than he would want) if its procedures are to be competently carried out and its conclusions falsifiable. Simplification may be the price of twentieth-century science. Generalizations have to be made. Many favourite correlations will have to be abandoned because they are untestable and therefore unfalsifiable. The most scientific graphology possible would make a slim textbook, and the character portraits it furnished would be arid and not very helpful, a list of traits which as in a computerized analysis may seem to contradict one another: gregarious, moody, irritable. These are the variables; to be of any use a graphological portrait is required to *integrate* them.

In so far as the terms used by Jung, Freud, Adler and other depth psychologists are standardized and offer verifiable hypotheses, behavioural psychology is at least as scientific as empirical psychology.[15] But it has to said that these older theories, constructed when psychology was a new discipline, are not nowadays considered to any degree scientific. Nevertheless they are much used — particularly in continental graphology, which commands general respect and some academic recognition. These graphologists recognize that there are many uncertainties and complexities in human behaviour and psychological attitudes, and the depth psychologists' scepticism of the scientific *Weltanschauung* appeals to them.

It is at this point that some graphologists may decide that graphology cannot or should not be regarded as a science. They may feel that scientific (testable) graphology is bad graphology, while good graphology, full of complex synthesis and reference to unconscious mental propensities, is bad science. They will not therefore want to suggest that their graphology is scientific, or advertise it as such. We need to look more closely at this point of view.

Graphology as an Art:

The Portrait

If graphology constitutes art, it does so in more than one way. In one sense art enters graphology despite our best efforts and even after rigorous scientific methods have been applied. In another seeing graphology as an art accommodates the reservations of the depth psychologists as described above. In a third sense it replaces the scientific in graphology altogether. In no sense does it match Freud's opinion of art, that 'it does not seek to be anything but an illusion'; that 'it makes no attempt at invading the realm of reality'.[16]

Each of these variations claims to show the truth about character. Each incidentally illustrates the relationship of graphology to science.

I shall look first at 'accidental' art. The first shift away from scientific method comes, as I have already suggested, after the list of correlations has been made. However meticulously this has been done, however sound and basic the correlations are, the graphologist may unwittingly introduce art when making the portrait. We have seen that if the analysis is to be presented to a client it must be put into comprehensible form; the character traits must be juxtaposed, interrelated, balanced out, and put under the kind of headings a client will need, such as social and reactive behaviour, working qualities, and so on. But the final portrait may deflect the ultimate achievement of graphology from science to art. With every intention of being objective in the way we deal with our data, our emotions, unconscious attitudes and creative impulses may be at work. The term we are forced to introduce here is subjectivity.

Our subjective viewpoints may be culturally shaped or conditioned by our particular dispositions and experiences, causing us to construct a hierarchy of interpretation which promotes emphasis on one characteristic at the expense of another. This may result in implicit moral judgement. The hierarchy problem is intensified by the fact that in order for the portrait to be as scientific as possible the balance of the personality has to be hierarchically conveyed! The selection of *dominants, secondary movements* and *miscellaneous movements* affects the construction of the portrait, since it puts emphasis on the writer's strongest and most evident characteristics.

It is crucial that these three groups of movements be unequivocally evident; that no one of normal visual ability could challenge the signs we decide upon. Even so, the groups must still vary within a margin of acceptability, the result being that no two portraits are exactly alike. The three categories of movement mentioned above are discussed more fully on page 155. Perhaps more than any other single aspect of graphological practice they pinpoint the *inability* of good graphology to meet the strictest criteria of science.

One way of reducing subjectivity in portrait writing is to take note of the predispositions found in our own handwriting. As I discuss on page 51, no Jungian therapist is allowed to practise until he or she has undergone psychotherapy. The problem of the subjective viewpoint and its basis is well illustrated by Freud's obsessional emphasis on sexuality and Adler's attention to the will to power. Were these purely theories, or were they the outcome of unresolved personal psychological trauma? Why were they made fundamental to the assessment of all the various psychic disorders encountered? While trying to make sure we analyse from no dubiously idiosyncratic basis, we can take comfort from the fact that even in the strictest of scientific theories there may lurk an unhappy childhood experience, or a stubborn blindness to all previous findings. Whether the insights born of such subjective promptings constitute irrational prejudice or genius is confirmed or falsified by testing. Anyone who wishes to see graphology established as a science will work towards laying agreed foundations rather than disturbing them by forming speculative conclusions. Others will want the artistic component of our practice to receive both recognition and judicious application.

Before leaving the struggles of scientifically-orientated graphology to exclude art from its practice, I would like to introduce briefly the modern notion that truth is perspectival. This philosophical belief holds that because we cannot get outside our human condition, and because we have no means of knowing what truth is except through our own meagre physical faculties and their technical brain-children, we are justified in spinning our own webs of belief and calling them truth. But this theory of knowledge does not allow incoherent belief systems to call themsevles truth. You won't find in its learned literature anything very kind about pseudo-sciences that cannot build webs because they have no foundational framework, no agreed basic assumptions. The criteria of empirical science remain the same whether we hold that our conclusions represent reality, how things real-ly are, or whether we believe them simply to represent our best findings, as corroborated by our shared observations and experience.

You will meet general medical practitioners, some natural scientists, a host of social scientists, and at least one dentist who call their practice an art. Don't be misled. They work within a strict disciplinary matrix, and it is only because they are thoroughly grounded in its fundamental assumptions that they feel free to allow themselves a little liberality of interpretation. This is not a luxury which any graphologist who claims to practise scientifically can abuse. If a graphologist answers 'yes' when asked if he or she is scientifically trained then there is no room for art. If on the other hand he or she hesitates, this is the point at which a graphologist is perhaps saying that a client can be helped more by art than by science, that it is the graphologist's unique insight, which may seem to have no place in a scientifically-orientated practice, that must work on the script.

Symbolism

I shall now consider graphology as positively-conceived art. Those who try to practise scientifically will dwell on well-attested correlations of handwriting traits with character traits, and will be content for the final portrait to state these in a properly organized but possibly bald way. But many graphologists are convinced that symbolism, as used for example in Pulver's zonal interpretation (see p. 53), best expresses what they want to say of a piece of writing, and throws great light on the character of the writer. Symbolism has long been used in graphology, and has contributed to an enriched understanding of human experience and attitudes, as it has done for other art forms. But is enriched understanding true understanding? Symbols, unless closely defined, are open to multiple interpretations. There is a broad and continuing debate on whether symbols and metaphors do actually reveal any truth at all. Scientifically-orientated graphologists may incline toward the view of the philosopher Thomas Hobbes, that understanding things metaphorically is not understanding them at all. But others who are most intensely aware of the complexity of human propensity and action find that symbols have more to do with the living character of truth than any correlation found valid by science.

It must be said at once that some forms of symbolism *can* be found valid by science. Very often the symbol can be re-expressed as testable variables, for example 'rivers' in writing are, in fact, irregular spacing. But many symbolic correlations are unscientific because they are untestable. They allow for diverse interpretation. In a closed system of metaphor, where definitions are strictly given and only one interpretation is possible, this may be avoided. But in most cases the symbolism is quite arbitrarily constructed.

One of the most powerful and sustained defences of symbolism as a form of knowledge was put forward by Jung. He found the origins of symbolic understanding in a complex psychophysical phenomenon, a finding by no means rejected by scientists interested in the functioning of the old (i.e. reptilian) brain of man.[17] He believed that many of our ideas had been stamped on the human brain for millions of years, and might only with great difficulty be articulated verbally.[18] After his break with Freud in 1913, Jung wanted it understood that his teachings were concerned with extremely complicated psychic contexts, which went far beyond and beneath a psychology that reduced everything to instinctual elements. He required that investigations should go beyond the boundaries of the individual's own relationships in experience: he asked that we look not only downwards and inwards to find out the truth about ourselves, but also 'backwards into the depths of time and down into the labyrinth of the psychological continuum'.[19] Many of these ideas came from the East, from concepts little understood in Europe. Jung had no qualms about quoting the inspiring notions of these ancient civilizations, and he introduced Eastern ideas defiantly to the West. He wrote: 'The thoughts of the old masters' — he meant Confucius and the revered, mountain-dwelling leaders of Chan Buddhism, and the preservers of the Tao — 'are of greater value to me than the philosophical prejudices of the Western mind'.[20] Jung impelled twentieth-century Europe to look to the past and to the far side of the world where, he said, 'People have trained their minds in introspective psychology for thousands of years, whereas we began with our psychology not even yesterday, but this morning'.[21]

There is a direct link between Jung's theories and graphology, since traits correlating with his four psychological types can be found in writing (p. 147 below). The French graphologist Ania Teillard was for thirty years a pupil of Jung, and in her book *L'Ame et L'Ecriture* she makes an understanding of psychology a requisite for being a sound graphologist. We are not concerned here with Jung's role as a psychologist, but with his findings as a student of ancient studies, in which Teillard also roots her psychology and graphology.[22] She shares his belief that symbols can lead to a constructive understanding of the truth. One of Jung's first and most admired findings was the T'ai Chi counter-balance of opposing poles (see p. 55 below). This was the inspiration for his terms *extrovert* and *introvert*. He believed that in thrusting forward into new practices and standards based on new knowledge humankind was discarding ancient wisdom, and he spent a lifetime illustrating how this was so.

Jung's phrase 'stamped on the human brain' does not suggest that he looked elsewhere than in the body for the spiritual dimension in humanity; indeed he offered the idea that matter and psyche are two aspects of the same substance.[23] I quoted earlier Jung's allusion to the spiritual and biological in humans. The psyche can be studied both by philosophical *materialists*, who think that the mind is nothing but brain activity, and *dualists*, who believe the mind is or is partly constituted by something quite apart from the flesh, and that the psyche is a non-natural (that is, spiritual) substance which can survive without the body. It is possible to talk of spiritual humanity without denying that the mind is the result of brain activity, just as it is possible to be very ambiguous indeed. It is not clear that Jung was suggesting that any part of human existence or experience was non-natural, that is, quite outside the many and varied processes of nature, but he certainly enjoyed mysteries and was content for them to remain as such.

Graphology is not, any more than is analytical psychology, going to be considered an occult-practice simply because it points to ancient psychic connections to support the idea that the range of human responses has not altered during humanity's existence as a species. Nevertheless it should be remembered that these associations are not always to our advantage, that just as in psychoanalysis we risk links with practices neither compatible with modern science nor generally culturally respectable. Do we pick over entrails and look for signs in the environment when there can be no possibility of a causal connection between sign and state of mind? This is certainly not true of graphology; causal connections can at least to some extent be immediately established, but this is how it may seem to some observers. Gellner holds that such recoiling could apply to Freudian slips and dream interpretation.[24] There is a clear analogy between word association, trait correlation, and the Babylonian practice of 'naming the devil' (whereby a magician would recite long lists of ghosts and devils by name to a 'possessed' victim, any one of which might (it was thought) be the cause of his or her sickness or distress. When its name was called out the evil spirit was unmasked and, dispossessed of its power to cause harm, vanished). Finding out truths about oneself or hitting on a deeply hidden problem might be thought to have a similar effect.

It may be that graphology is enriched by bringing in evidence of humanity's earliest forms of understanding, since the implication is that such understanding will be at a more profound level than is our modern, rational thought. This would be the basis for interpreting handwriting through the use of symbols. Some graphologists may choose to call themselves interpreters of symbols. If so, they must either bring to their work (through closed systems of metaphor) the meticulous consistency and psychological understanding found in the work of Teillard, or declare themselves unscientific practitioners, who use evidence in their work which cannot be tested.

Intuition

It is one thing to argue for a method of graphology which can be validated, but quite another to deny completely graphology's status as a study or taught doctrine as established by Michon. To qualify as a study in our present culture a practice must have a methodology. Relying on intuitive hunches about a script, or claiming to use psychic gifts or any other untestable esoteric divination in handwriting analysis is to be unable to say from which specific traits in the client's writing one's conclusions are deduced. Such practice does not answer the prime claim of graphology: that *particular handwriting* traits indicate *particular character* traits.

Intuitive hypotheses about particular correlations or methods of 'divining' mental or physical states from handwriting take the path to scientific validation on their own account. To do this they will have to construct testable hypotheses, and for this to be possible the procedures used must not only be within nature, compatible with our known physics, but must be observably so. It is to be expected that scientific practices outside orthodox graphology might prove valid diagnostic tools. For example, the testing of physiological electrocommunication channels to measure currents in script (rhythm, spontaneity, dynamism, libido etc.) would constitute a neuroscientific investigation of the writing process. It would not be orthodox graphology and it would not claim to be, but like Pophal's work it could help to validate the claims of graphology. All intuitions must be testable if they are to sustain a repeatable procedure.

'Well,' says the intuitive graphologist, 'my way of interpreting handwriting has been corroborated — by all my satisfied clients.' This kind of remark is the cause of the widespread dismissal of graphology by rational people. Interpretations that are the outcome of 'just knowing', with no reasons or correlations given, not only lay themselves open to the charge of being chance successes, but damage the status of careful orthodox practice.

The television programme investigating graphology (*Q.E.D.*, BBC 2, 12th April, 1989) implied at one stage that many non-graphologists receive 'impressions' from handwriting and so are able to distinguish different types of writers, or even particular traits. This is to a limited extent true, and its truth may be founded in man's early visual signalling systems, as discussed in relation to Jung's theory of ancient and now almost subliminal understanding. But such perception is unscientific since there is no way of knowing if the conclusions are constant, shared, testable, or repeatable. If unfairly pushed even trained graphologists may resort to relying on this form of perception, but it is a great mistake and does nothing for graphology's reputation.

Bradley's *99 Studies* gives an example of this.[25] In tests trained graphologists distinguished genuine suicide notes from fake ones, but they could not say why. They received pictures or resemblances of despair, negativity, self-hatred and so on. Such pictures and images are very unreliable; they do not depend on accepted symbolic interpretations, and we know that even those can be indeterminate. We can never be sure of the basis in meaning or experience of this kind of resemblance, and there is a danger that if we trust it we could find one feature of the writing resembles a great many incompatible things. Consider a foreign visitor newly arrived and looking at road signs. How would he know what to expect if the correlations hadn't been explained to him? (Especially if he came upon the road-up sign, so often depicted as a man lying upside down holding an umbrella over his head). A direct example from graphology is 'rivers'. We might see all kinds of rivers in script: how do I know if you're seeing a river, and exactly where? Irregular word spacing, on the other hand, constitutes a non-perspectival variable.

Intuitive interpreters may be getting very cross with me by now: they are certain they are right. But my explanation is given only to emphasize the fact that their judgements are not the result of eye-training in relation to specific movements as are those of orthodox or scientifically-orientated

graphologists. Their intuition or psychic insight might in fact be explained
as unclassified memory or pre-verbal signalling, or might be the result of
a force outside the scope of most people's sensory faculties. The intuitive
interpreter who 'just knows' may indeed be in possession of such non-
sensory knowledge.

It may also be true that the current scientific viewpoint is totally
misguided, and that a later culture will admit this. There is plenty of
dissatisfaction within scientific disciplines now, though it is noticeable
that most of it comes from those whose tested conclusions are not
accepted. It was there in Freud's day, and he defended the scientific
Weltanschauung against it: 'There is a good deal of exaggeration in this
criticism of science. It is not true that it staggers blindly from one
experiment to another, that it replaces one error by another'.[26]
Nevertheless, the so-called paranormal which stands outside our
knowledge may one day be included within it. There is no way of
knowing whether this is possible or not; indeed it is difficult to see how
the purely sensory faculties with which we seem to be equipped are going
to find out if such knowledge exists. But only a fool would say that all
possible answers are obtainable through our current science, and there
are few such fools in science. The only thing that those who follow
orthodox and scientifically-orientated graphological procedures would
ask is that those who 'just know' do not call themselves orthodox
graphologists or give the impression that their work is sanctioned by the
graphological bodies cited at the end of this book.

Forming a Conclusion

I have given several different viewpoints on graphology, and it should
now be possible for readers to form an individual opinion. I began this
discussion by pointing out that our current culture demands that we
account rationally for what we think and do, and that we give this
account within an empirical framework. Neither our reasoning nor our
causal explanations may be sufficient to justify our current belief system,
but we have not found anything to replace them or to show they are not
necessary. Even the most pragmatic of conclusions — 'we don't know
why it works but it works' — is the result of testing. The testing
constitutes the methodology, and within it lies the reasoning and the
explanation for our beliefs.

It is quite conceivable that this framework of belief might change. The
limits of science are honestly marked by those best placed to understand
them, such as Nobel Prize-winning scientist Peter Medawar.[27] But the
rapid advance of Western science and our understanding of the physical

construction of the world, including ourselves as natural objects, speaks loudly and persuasively for its methods. This general viewpoint is not going to change in our lifetime.

I have not said that graphology is or can be an exact science. The position seems to me to be that meticulous research into graphological indicators or organic functional disorders and particular states of diseases might be equated with the scientific status of medicine. But graphological indicators of character traits, dealing as they do with the complexities of human behaviour and our evaluations of them, cannot be any more scientific than empirical psychology. Research into the *causal* mechanisms of character states and of particular handwriting traits puts our understanding of graphology into the domain of experimental psychology. Here are to be found the firmest foundations for orthodox graphology, but as I have said earlier, the part of our study which could be validated in this way is limited.

With such limitations and possibilities in mind, we can approach the study of graphology with an informed, critical and evaluative attitude. We can make our judgements with caution, checking the evidence for each correlation but remembering that all scientific conclusions on matters of fact are at best well corroborated, never conclusive.

References

1. G.W. Allport, *Studies in Expressive Movement* (New York, 1933).
2. Karl Popper, *Conjectures and Refutations: The Growth of Scientific Knowledge* (Routledge and Kegan Paul, 1963, p. 37).
3. M. Wilson, *Case Study of a Brain Tumour.* (Published by the British Institute of Graphologists in the series *Monographs in Graphology*, 1988.)
4. N. Bradley, *99 Studies in Handwriting and Related Topics* (Nigel Bradley, 1988, p. 68). Available from N. Bradley, 91 Hawksley Avenue, Chesterfield, Derbyshire S40 4TJ.
5. *Ibid.*, p. 95.
6. A brief shortlist of studies testing graphology's central claim: H.A. Williams and G. Stuparich, *Validity and Reliability of Handwriting Analysis* (San José State University, California, 1989). An unpublished paper, presented at the British Institute of Graphologists Symposium, University of Cambridge.
   B. Nevo, *Scientific Aspects of Graphology: A Handbook* (Springfield, Illinois: Charles C. Thomas, 1986).
   D. Lester, *The Relation of Handwriting to Personality and Psychopathology. The Psychological Basis of Handwriting Analysis* (Chicago: Nelson-Hall, 1981).
   O. Lockowandt, *Present Status of the Investigation of Handwriting Psychology as a Diagnostic Method* (Bielefeld, Germany: Paedogogische Höheschule, Westfalen — Lippe. Abt., 1976).

7. R. Pophal and E. Dunker, *Slow Motion Studies of Handwriting Movements* (Z. exp. Angew, Psychol. 1960, 7, 76–99).

8. For example, Roehampton College, London. Up-to-date information is available from the British Institute of Graphologists.

9. Margaret Gullan-Whur, *What Your Handwriting Reveals* (Aquarian Press, 1984, p. 23).

10. Dr Patricia Wellingham-Jones, P.O. Box 238, Tehama, California 96090, U.S.A.

11. Jolande Jacobi, *The Psychology of C.G. Jung* (Routledge and Kegan Paul, 1969).

12. Sigmund Freud, *Introductory Lectures on Psychoanalysis (1915–16)*, 2 vols. (Pelican Books, 1973, vol. 2, p. 211).

13. Ernest Gellner, *The Psychoanalytic Movement* (Granada, 1985, pp. 187–91).

14. Freud, vol. 2, p. 34.

15. C.G. Jung, *Psychological Types*. From *The Collected Works*, vol. 6 (Routledge and Kegan Paul, 1979, p. 90).

16. Freud, vol. 2, p. 196.

17. Carl Sagan, *The Dragons of Eden* (Hodder and Stoughton, 1979). *See also* Margaret Gullan-Whur, *The Four Elements*, Appendix A.

18. Jung's most accessible work on this subject is *Man and His Symbols* (Penguin, 1990).

19. C.G. Jung, *Psychology and the East* (Routledge and Kegan Paul, 1982, p. 11).

20. *Ibid.*, p. 203.

21. C.G. Jung, *Analytical Psychology (The Tavistock Lectures)* (Routledge and Kegan Paul, 1953).

22. Ania Teillard, *L'Ame et L'Écriture* (Éditions Traditionelles, 1983).

23. Jacobi, p. 62.

24. Gellner, p. 193.

25. Bradley, p. 101.

26. Freud, vol. 2, p. 211.

27. Peter Medawar, *The Limits of Science* (Oxford University Press, 1986).

I
Form Level:
The General Quality of the Writing

Glancing at a piece of handwriting for the first time is rather like meeting someone new. We are bound to be aware of a unique essence: we receive impressions which, because they are unconcerned with reason or cause, evaporate quickly on further acquaintance. Those first almost animal sensations may be recalled at will by some of us, but others are so keen to find out more by means of speech or deliberate observation that a vital, fleeting means of assessment is gone for ever.

It is important not to let this happen with handwriting. That first glimpse must be consciously registered, because however subjective our response must necessarily be, it will be hard to recapture it later. The coldness, the direct appeal, or the sense of chaos which emanates from handwriting, is real. It is also the only intuitive assessment we shall make in our analysis: all that follows is the result of systematic observation, and is a process which can be learned. The first impression, however, cannot.

In the first part of this workbook we shall be training our eyes to recognize overall movements in the writing, looking — as Klages suggests — at the individual's whole face rather than noting down its features. Each of the following writing samples illustrates one particular aspect only, and to avoid any confusion I have written that aspect in the caption below each sample.

We must never feel that we have to make a cut and dried assessment. Where should we be if we could not say, *'fairly* good-looking' or *'usually* blotchy in complexion, *but not always'*, or 'a lovely face *spoiled* by dyed hair'? We must make ample use of moderating adjectives, and whilst this book can only include a few rather obvious examples, remember that these are the exception, not the rule.

Harmony
In this assessment we *consider the writing as a picture*. Are its component

parts well-blended, or do some aspects seem harshly exaggerated? Is
there one movement which regularly 'spoils' the flow? Is the writing well-
proportioned and clear, or is there a sudden contraflow testifying to a lack
of harmony within the mind of the writer? Is it gracefully simple, or
fussily embellished?

We must be very careful. The picture may be a copy, not genuine at all.
Its apparent harmony or elegance may be a calculated eradication of
natural movements: the writing is at best an art form and at worst a mask
or a wig. We shall deal with this difficult aspect of graphology thoroughly
as we progress through Section I, but it suggests at once why
graphologists find beauty in less predictable writing.

Crépieux-Jamin considered harmonious writing to indicate 'the highest
moral bravery', a term little used today and one which recalls the
ecclesiastical origins of graphology. He also remarked that he had only
ever encountered — and he lived to be 80 — ten very harmonious samples
of writing! But his belief that complete harmony testified to complete
agreement amongst the different parts of the character is consistent with
the modern belief that a high degree of self-awareness produces self-
acceptance and stability of character.

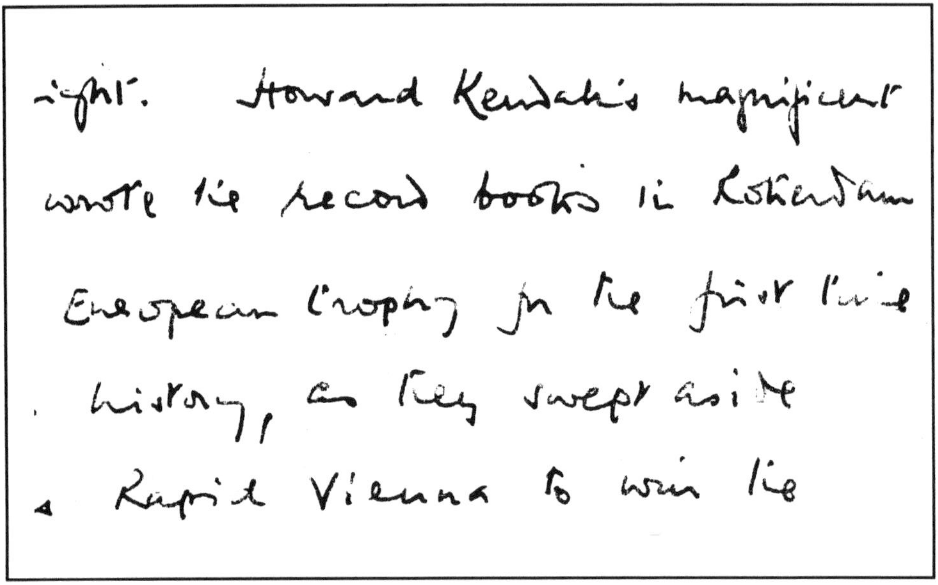

Figure 2   Generally harmonious

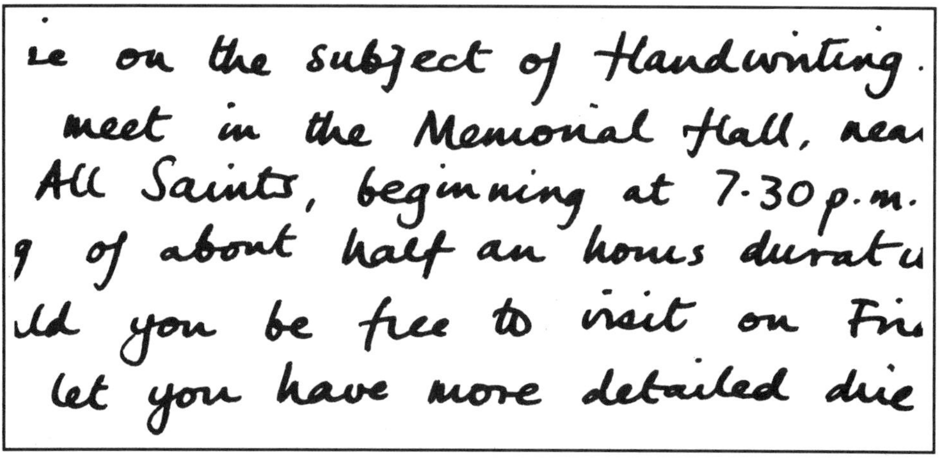

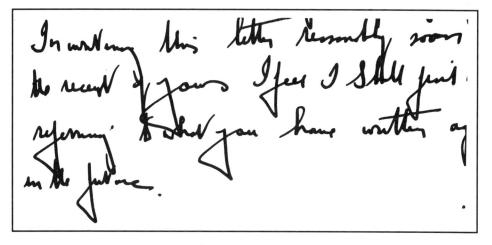

Figure 3   Generally harmonious

Figure 4   Inharmonious

Once in a while you may think you have encountered very harmonious writing. Beware. As with falling in love, the beauty may lie in your eyes only, and the writing reflect your ideal. Conversely, you may dislike the appearance of certain writing on equally subjective grounds. Test it by not only looking for exaggerated or contraflow movements, but by all the other criteria of Form Level.

On the scale of 1–5 used by some graphologists in assessing Form Level, be wary of giving grade 1 for **harmony**. In some respects this quality is a matter of first impression, but it requires a second glance.

Inharmonious writing is easy to recognize. It disturbs the eye and the mind with its discordance: we say it is ugly because something in its expression points to a lack of inner peace, not because it is merely untidy or crudely formed — **unorganized**.

Most writing, like most people, is averagely harmonious. And any individual may write with greater harmony at one time than another. Start looking at other samples, making tentative assessments.

Originality

Assessment for the general appearance or Form Level of the writing includes the degree of originality shown. Again, we must be careful not to admire excessively decorated letter forms, which show a love of (sometimes vulgar) visual adornment, rather than a truly creative spirit.

Originality is shown by the presence of strokes or *letter forms which the writer could never have been taught* in school or in calligraphy classes. These letter formations, or ways of linking letters or words, indicate a mind which takes fresh and independent paths, extending its unique vision of life into ideas or action. (It must follow that in some circumstances uniqueness of vision becomes insanity! None the less, the 'originality' grading would be high.)

The small quantities of originality which most of us show in our writing do not as a rule diminish its legibility. The purpose of all writing is to communicate, and originality becomes distortion at the point when it cannot be read. Earlier generations disliked unconventional letter forms as much as they disapproved of rebellious behaviour: older people still

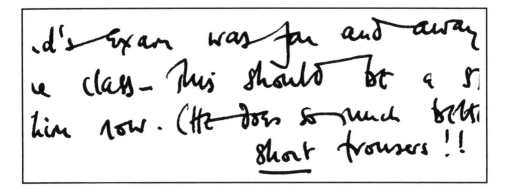

Figure 5 Originality

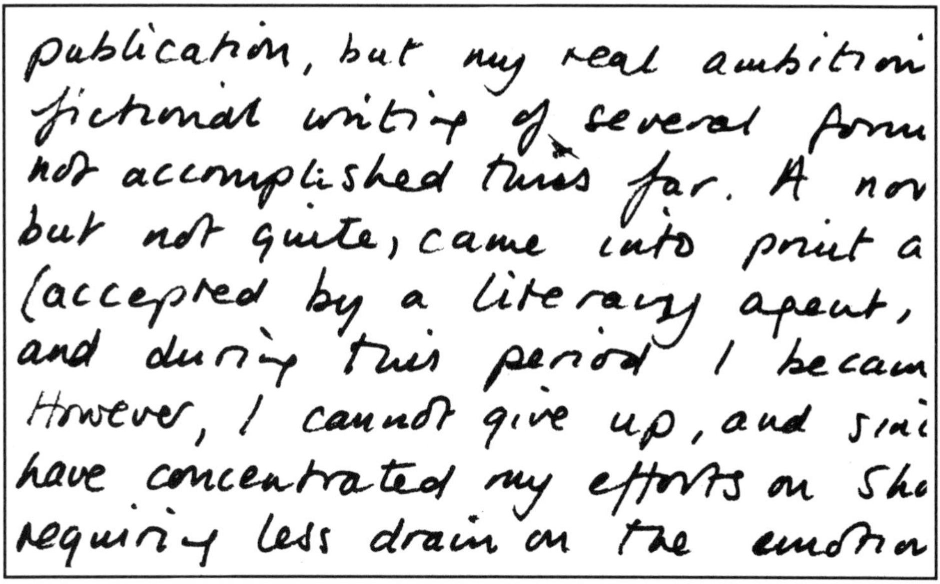

publication, but my real ambition
fictional writing of several form
not accomplished this far. A nov
but not quite, came into print a
(accepted by a literary agent,
and during this period I becam
However, I cannot give up, and sinc
have concentrated my efforts on sho
requiring less drain on the emotion

Figure 6 Some originality

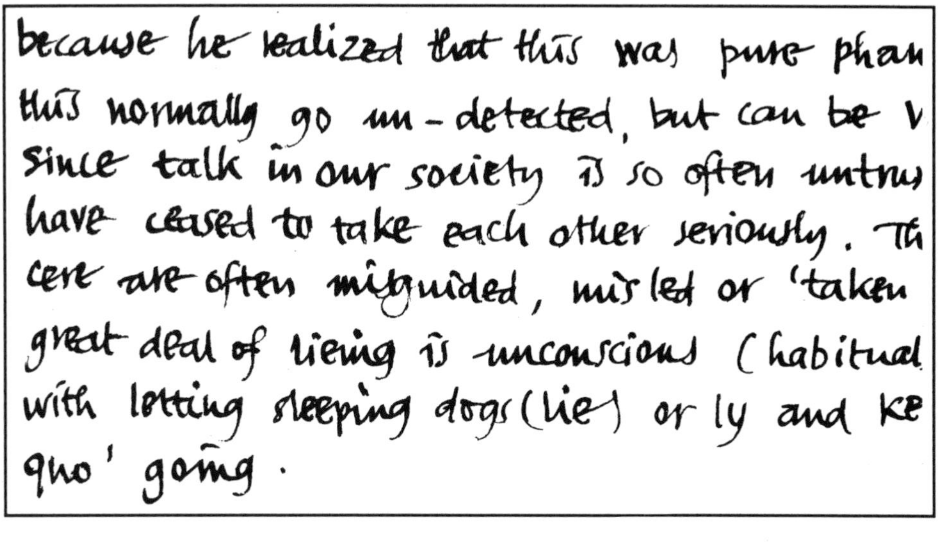

because he realized that this was pure phan
this normally go un-detected, but can be v
since talk in our society is so often untru
have ceased to take each other seriously. Th
cert are often misguided, misled or 'taken
great deal of lieing is unconscious (habitual
with letting sleeping dogs (lie) or ly and ke
quo' going.

Figure 7 Calligraphic (see also Fig. 101)

tell of their agonized efforts to produce good copybook script, and I am shown with pride the stereotyped results, from which all individuality has been stripped. Sad.

Yet small idiosyncrasies in the writing have always been noted, and considered a means of identification almost as certain as fingerprints. But not quite: in *Twelfth Night*, Olivia's were successfully forged:

> By my life, this is my lady's hand! These be her very C's, her U's and her T's; and thus she makes her great P's. It is, in contempt of question, her hand.

Writing which is mannered or artificial springs from a mind which contains a ready-made vision of a beautiful order in all things. Such a mind may be superficially elegant, but its vision is totally conscious, and we receive no sense of a blending between the inner (unconscious) life, and the outer strivings. The inner life is hidden behind a mask, the *persona* or public image through which the writer lives and by which he wants to be recognized. When **calligraphic** script is used for purposes other than illustrating, the writer is building and projecting an image for himself. He may also, in rare cases, be setting out deliberately to deceive or confuse.

Lack of originality in writing shows a desire to conform, and this is as

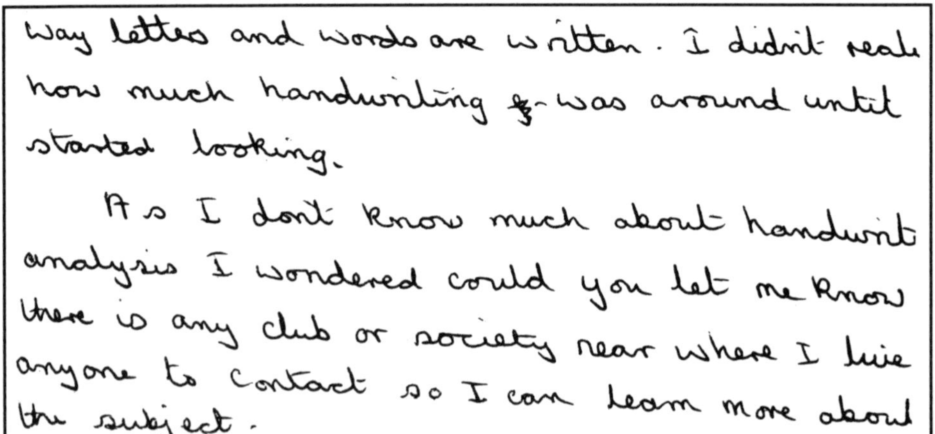

Figure 8 Copybook

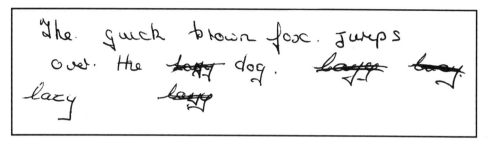

Figure 9 Unorganized

true of calligraphic writing as of **copybook** script (Fig. 8), where the writer does not stray from the formations he was taught at school. But whereas the calligraphic writer wants to conform to an ideal of beauty or style, the copybook writer is still trying to conform to the standards of those who had authority or influence over him when he was young. He does not think very much for himself, and prefers to follow the guidelines others give him. This is probably also true of his manner of dress and the way he runs his life generally: he is a conformist.

The most frequently found writing of all is that in which a glimmering of originality appears to flicker and is then immediately quenched, hauled back into line through self-discipline, apathy or fear. (If the writer of Fig. 8 were to be told that his w is unusually formed or his i-dot is comma-shaped, he would probably try to correct them both.) Such writing may be **pseudo-copybook**.

Make a tentative assessment of the originality in Figs. 2–4, using a scale of 1 (original) to 5 (unoriginal) if you like.

Organization

Few graphologists attempt to analyse the handwriting of children under 12 years old, simply because at that age writing does not usually flow sufficiently automatically from the brain through the fingertips to the paper. It sometimes happens that later in life, too, handwriting shows such effort of awkwardness in its composition that it is impossible to analyse. Illiteracy, illness, slow adaptation to a new culture and language, the use of drugs which affect brain processes and a pathological fear or dislike of the writing process (Writer's Cramp or Disturbance), can all cause such stasis in the writing.

The example in Fig. 9 was given to me to analyse by the mother of two young children. I believe that her lack of graphic ease was reinforced by a

Discover Graphology

terror of being graded which dated back to her schooldays, and here is another lesson for graphologists to learn. A gentle approach and a clear wish to help, not criticize, should be the cornerstone of our professional code, which is one reason why I personally do not add up points when assessing.

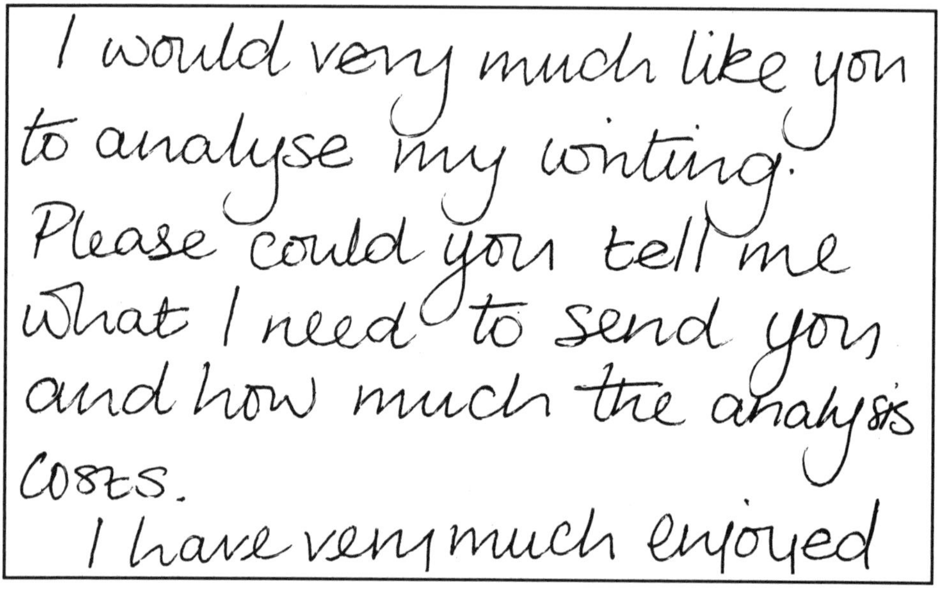

Figure 10 Organized

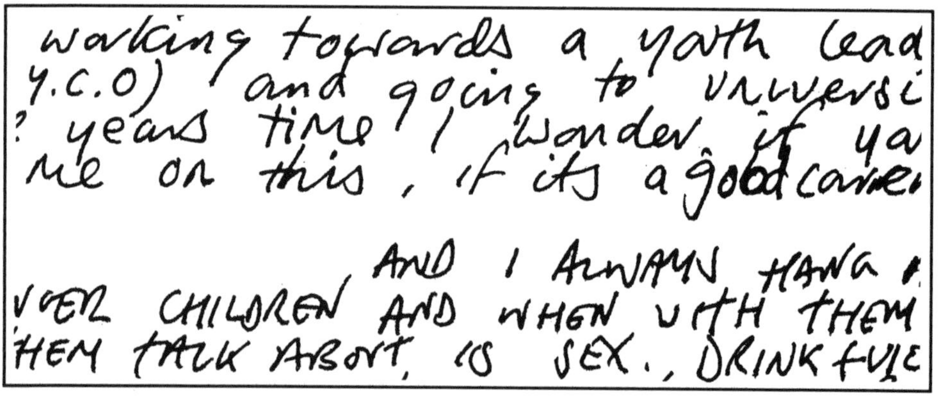

Figure 11 Progressively disorganized

Organized writing moves in conjunction with the thought processes, fluently translating the words in the mind to paper. Most writing which is

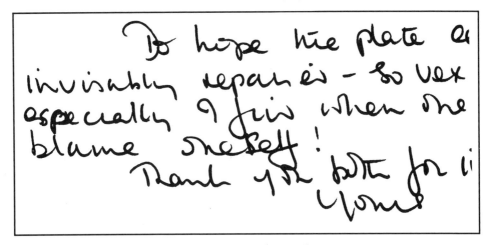

Figure 12 Organized

set down for others to read is reasonably organized, though from the analyst's point of view it must have at least the freedom of movement of the average 13 or 14-year-old's script. We must not confuse organization with tidiness: **organization** *means the mind and the pen working well together,* and has been described as *graphic ease.*

When there is a good degree of liaison between the thought processes and the act of writing them down, the writing appears to move smoothly across the paper, without any apparent effort. Thus the use of capital letters is not an organized formation, but in graphological terms a *disorganized* one. Whereas the writing in Fig. 9 had never become automatic and was *un*organized, the script in Fig. 11 changes from a fair level of organization to a graphic form more akin to drawing than handwriting — capitals.

Writing which previously showed a high degree of organization may become disorganized and lose much of its harmony. This may be temporary, and due to boredom, tiredness or difficult physical writing conditions. This commonsense cause is often ignored in graphology books, yet most of us can make rough notes which are illegible even to ourselves, and if we try to write on a fast-moving train, our script may look as though we are having a nervous breakdown. This is temporarily disorganized writing. If you suspect as much, *ask.* I was told of a hospital consultant whose tremulous, broken writing was giving his colleagues anxiety, since doctors know that such writing can be caused by illness, physical debility, senility or any damage to the nervous system. Eventually another doctor plucked up courage to mention it. 'Yes,' said the consultant, 'I really must stop writing up my notes on my pigskin briefcase.'

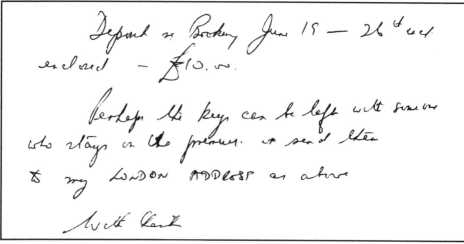

Figure 13 Disorganized

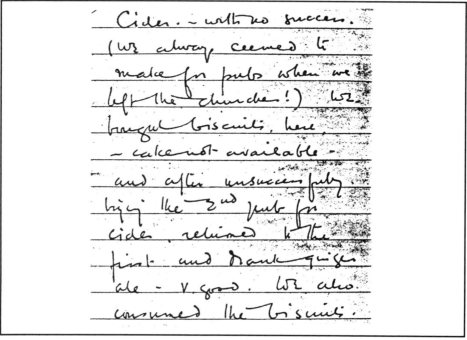

Figure 14 Spontaneous

If no obvious explanation is given, we must assume that the disorganization is due to one of the more serious causes above. The motor functions of the brain suffer from wear and tear, and this is reflected in the writing. We are talking here of biological processes, and this is perhaps the place to differentiate between the *brain*, which is a physical organ, and the *mind*, which represents the activity of the brain as a whole and is thus the *result* of brain events.

Some writing formations are caused by physical, not psychological states.

Spontaneity

This quality is a combination of speed and vitality, and yet it is neither. It concerns what is going on in the writer's mind before he begins to write: it indicates his willingness or otherwise to commit himself to paper, and thereby to the world of public action. And so in assessing spontaneity we tend to look at the gateway of entry into the writing process — the left-hand side of the words — and see *with what willingness the writer projects himself into life,* and then check as to whether the initial enthusiasm is sustained.

Reckless indeed is the character which hurls himself into world space without caution or subsequent watchfulness, so beyond a certain degree of unconstrained, natural movement, spontaneity can become a negative factor in the writing. If you are handing out points for this section, anything beyond a consistently forward-moving impulse which the French call *accelerated* writing, does not score full marks.

Writing which appears to skim across the page at great speed, leaving letters and words unfinished or drawn out into a **thread**, may show

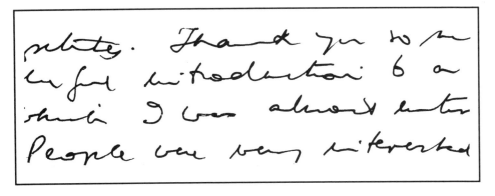

Figure 15   Over-spontaneous

excessive spontaneity in the form of impatience, imprudence, avoidance of responsibility or hyperactivity. On the other hand, it may not, so until we have learned the small signs of groups of signs which indicate these qualities, let us simply look on such writing as over-spontaneous.

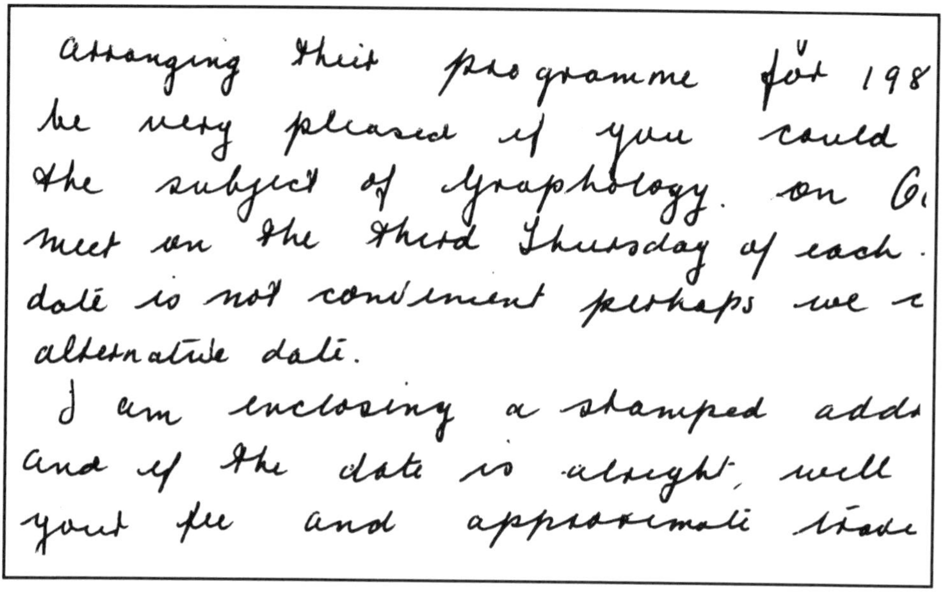

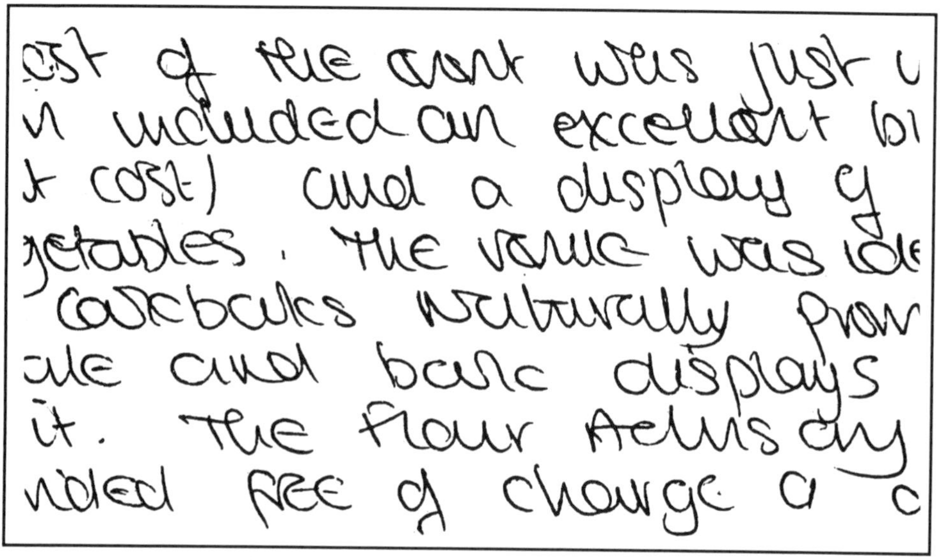

Figures 16 and 17 Inhibited spontaneity

Let us remember, too, that such impetus may not be habitual. We say, 'I must dash off a note', and that is exactly what we do. It does not mean that we dash off everything we write, or that this psychological state is habitual. We must remember to judge each piece of writing as springing from one particular moment in time, and to recall Michon's qualifying comment on page 8.

Some of us are, however, far more prone to spontaneous action than are others, and when we show a habitual tendency to implement our thoughts and feelings without reserve, spontaneity may be said to be characteristic. (Charles Darwin noted that such behaviour in babies and young animals was a highly individual matter remarkably soon after birth.)

It is normal — and in psychological terms this covers vast areas of our behaviour — to venture into world space and to check constantly that it is safe to move forward. This is what animals do. Most of us act with guarded spontaneity, with neither the intrepid enthusiasm of the writers in Figs. 14 and 15, nor the measured and deliberate reflection indicated in Figs. 18 and 19. If you like, we drive quite fast with the brakes on.

We have already learned that calligraphic or embellished writing cannot be spontaneous, since it is formed consciously and deliberately. This is especially true when it is carefully formed, as opposed to habitual and slightly negligent formations such as we saw in Fig. 7.

Very slow writing of all kinds shows a lack of spontaneity, but **calm** writing can indicate caution without any severe restraint on enthusiasm.

Many graphologists refer to spontaneity in the writing without first defining it. It is not always easy to assess, but following the script with a dry point, as recommended by G. Beauchataud, may help find negative, inhibiting factors. Have another look at some of the samples we have seen so far.

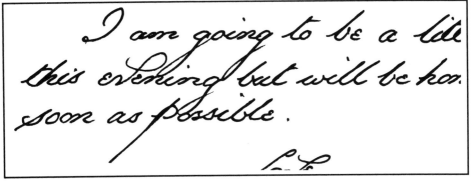

Figure 18 Unspontaneous

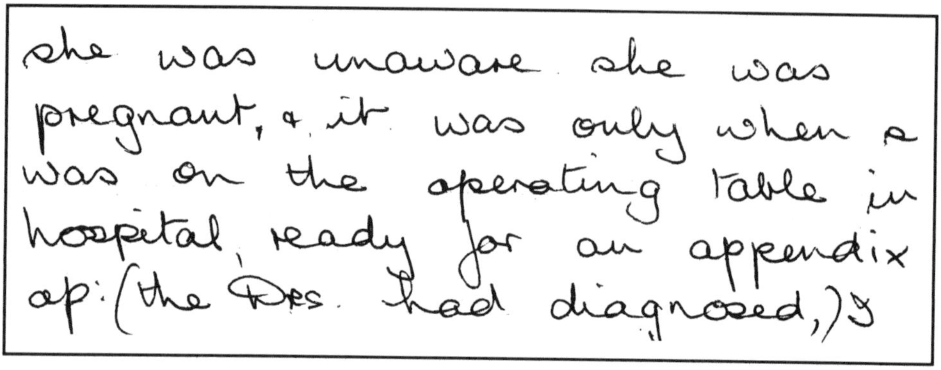

> she was unaware. she was
> pregnant, & it was only when a
> was on the operating table in
> hospital, ready for an appendix
> op: (the Drs. had diagnosed,) I

Figure 19 Calm, adequately spontaneous

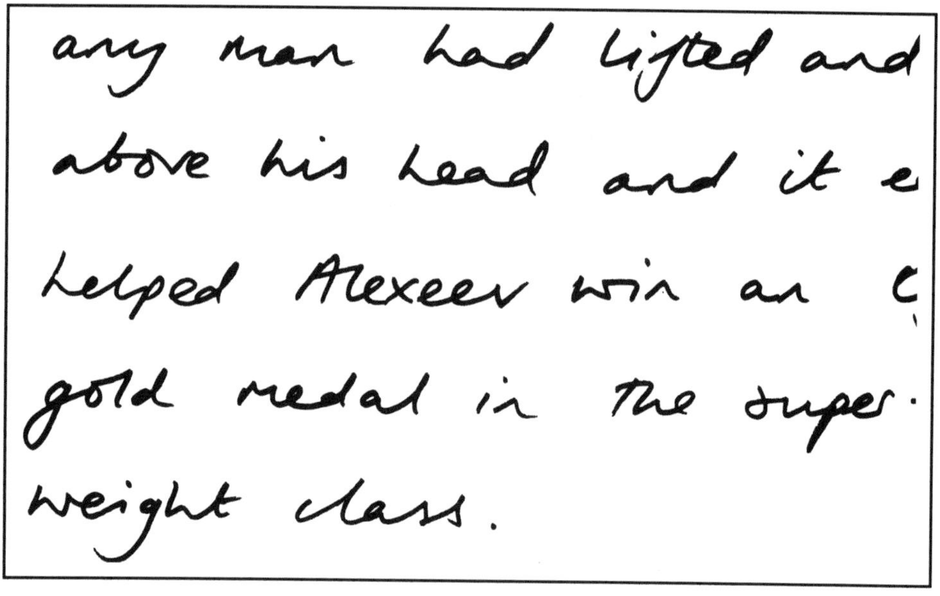

> any man had lifted and
> above his head and it e
> helped Alexeev win an C
> gold medal in The super.
> weight class.

Figure 20 Dynamism — intense life force

Dynamism

We are looking here for energy, but of the spirit rather than the body. *Writing charged with an intense life force* owes its vitality to mental rather than physical qualities, and dynamism is not necessarily found in the handwriting of those who appear energetic. A sportsman's writing, for instance, may show instead a remarkable degree of organization, since he actually uses more control than spontaneity in his achievements. The little old lady, full of indomitable courage after five bereavements and six major operations, manifests the extent of her psychic energy in vigorous unrestrained pen movements.

To Freud *libido* was solely sexual dynamism, but Jung extended its scope to an appetite (or *desire*, which is its meaning) for many other of life's good things. In considering it as *energy*, he hoped to give it the quantitative properties of physics: he believed it should be measured rather than judged. This idea has an interesting relevance to graphology, and whilst Ania Teillard, as a pupil of Jung, looks for strong, progressive, regressive or blocked libido, we can also bear in mind that writing becomes charged with dynamism on those occasions when desire or excitement is aroused. Therefore, while learning to recognize it in handwriting, we must be careful not to impute a low or high quantity of dynamism to the individual from one sample.

It is true that some people retain a zest for living while others, faced with a similar series of circumstances, seem unable to conjure the same resilience of spirit. The euphoria and enthusiasm shown in Fig. 20 may

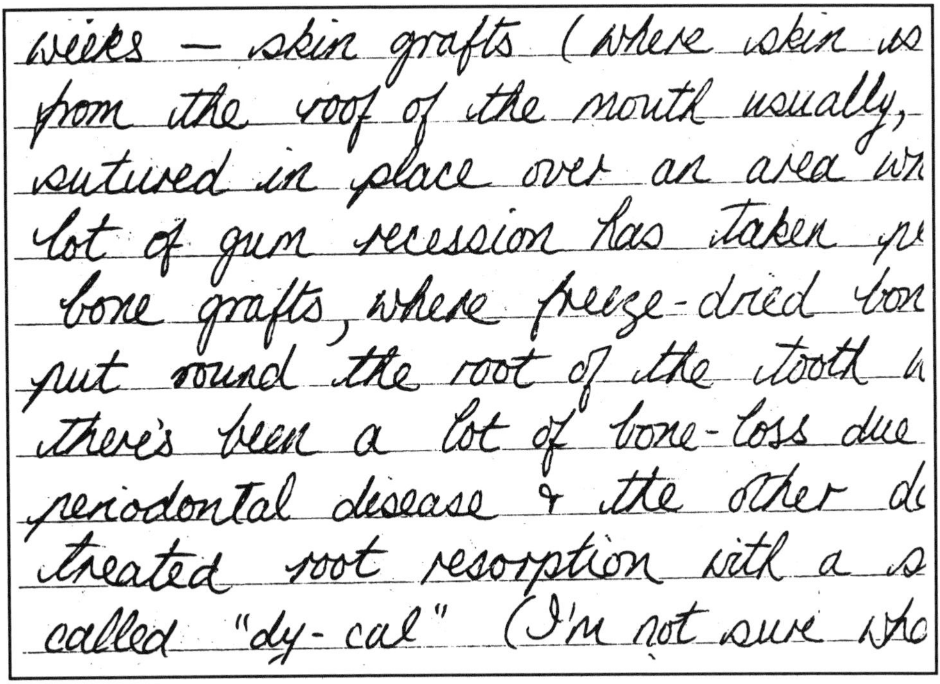

Figure 21   Fairly dynamic, resolute

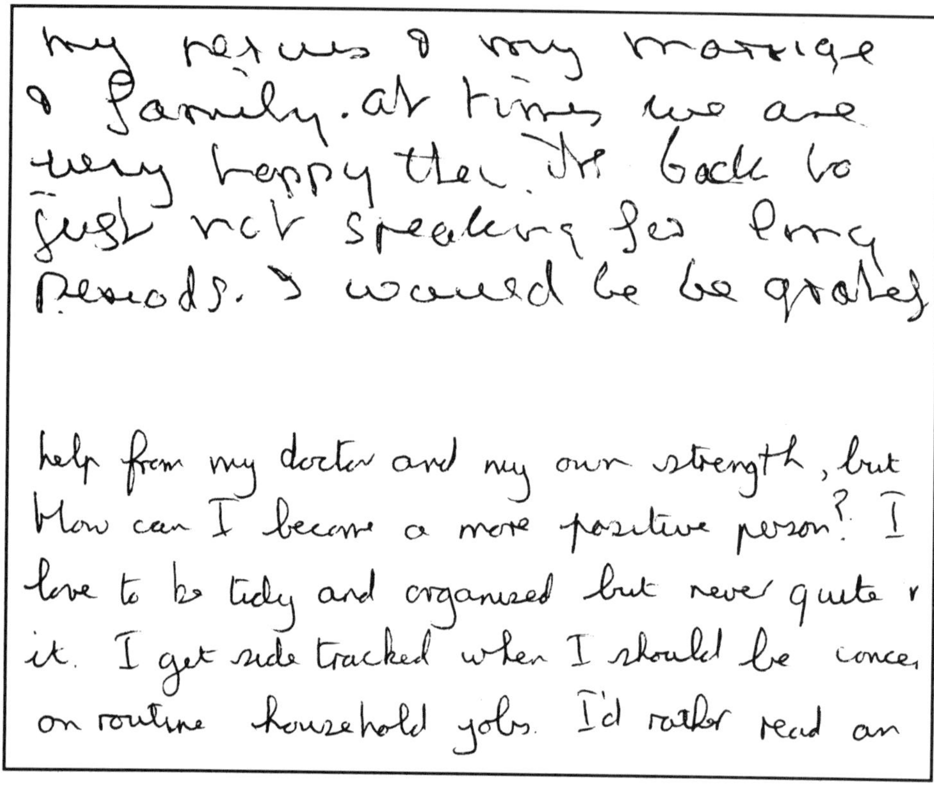

my nerves & my marriage
& family. at times we are
very happy then its back to
just not speaking for long
periods. I would be be grate[s]

help from my doctor and my own strength, but
How can I become a more positive person? I
love to be tidy and organised but never quite r
it. I get side tracked when I should be conce,
on routine household jobs. I'd rather read an

Figures 22 and 23   Low dynamism

not contain the same consistently energized endurance as the somewhat less dynamic attitude shown in Fig. 21, but on the other hand it may. We need to see plenty of samples if we are going to measure dynamism fairly.

Where resolution or desire seems scarcely maintained, the writing has a appearance of apathy or monotony. Sometimes it is light or faint, the lack of vigour or enthusiasm in the mind almost preventing the words from imprinting themselves at all. Again, we need to know whether external circumstances brought this about, or whether this is the normal appearance of the writing. Low dynamism in the writing of a teenager can be a sad indication of low hope in life, but it can also be a sign of the temporary outgrowing of strength. We all know the need to 'recharge our batteries', so be careful not to impute to temperament what truly belongs to biology.

Some graphologists believe that rough, textured paper is preferred by those who are of consistently dynamic and strong-willed character, because such people like a challenge — a resistance to overcome. I am not convinced by this — only a small percentage of the population actually chooses what to write on — but test this hypothesis for yourself.

Many of us show a similar attitude and level of dynamism to our degree of spontaneity. Our energy and enthusiasm, initially strong if our childhood has given us a cheerful expectation of life, becomes inhibited by a greater or lesser quantity of anxiety. We become slightly (or severely) crushed by the difficulties we experience, although the crushing and the experiences may be in no way comparable. So, our writing shows *inhibition or hesitancy*, and this fluctuates between the writing of a joyful and unrestrained personal letter, and the testing circumstances of a tedious report or a letter we dislike having to write.

Dynamism in writing is a measure of human life force. We assess it as high, middling or low, without judging at this stage whether it is used positively or negatively.

Rhythm
This subtle and as yet inadequately defined aspect of handwriting was first described by Klages in his *Handschrift und Charakter* as the periodic

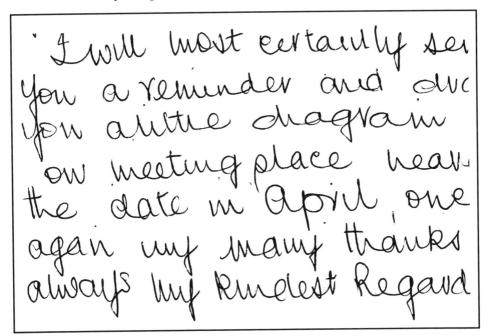

Figure 24 Inhibited dynamism

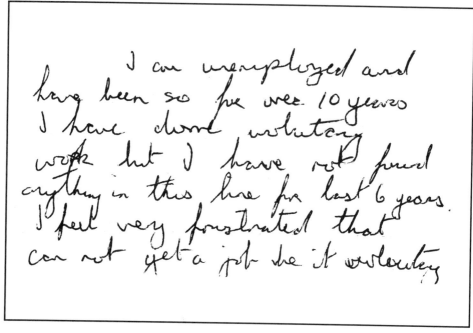

Figure 25   Disturbed, uncoordinated rhythm

reproduction of certain phenomena. These movements in the writing occurred in similar intervals which were never exact repetitions, so that although the rhythm they formed could be called a *graphic pulse*, it was not comparable to the ticking of a clock.

A lively, co-ordinated rhythm in the writing has since been taken by all graphologists who have studied it to mean *psychic energy — the radiation of a well-integrated personality.* Now, this definition means that the response between the conscious and the unconscious functions of the mind is in perfect accord, a state which Jung called *individuation*. It is the goal of psychotherapists of all schools to bring themselves and their clients to such a point of self-knowledge and self-acceptance, but in realistic terms they have as much chance as a Buddhist has of reaching supreme enlightenment within one lifetime. Individuation is a goal best kept as lying just over the next hill: always to be sought, but without positive expectation of success. John Beck calls rhythm 'a first-class indicator of an individual's capacity to integrate his physical, emotional and intellectual drives, and his ability to find a balance between these drives'.

To a large extent this assessment is made through the harmony of the writing, since we search there for signs and movements indicating excessive emphasis on one particular aspect of living. We have already seen that stress and conflict reduce harmony, organization, spontaneity and dynamism in the writing, and the lack of a regular movement in the script means that it cannot be described as rhythmic. Obviously stress is present in Fig. 25 — try tracing the words over with a dry point to share the writer's low state in all the qualities we have discussed so far. Sadly, poor rhythm is not hard to spot, nor is it uncommon. But it seems that stress affects the motor impulses of the brain, so that the appearance in writing will be exactly the same as that caused by physical trauma. We must be very sure that the disturbed rhythm or lack of co-ordination is not the result of arthritis or another disability, asking if necessary.

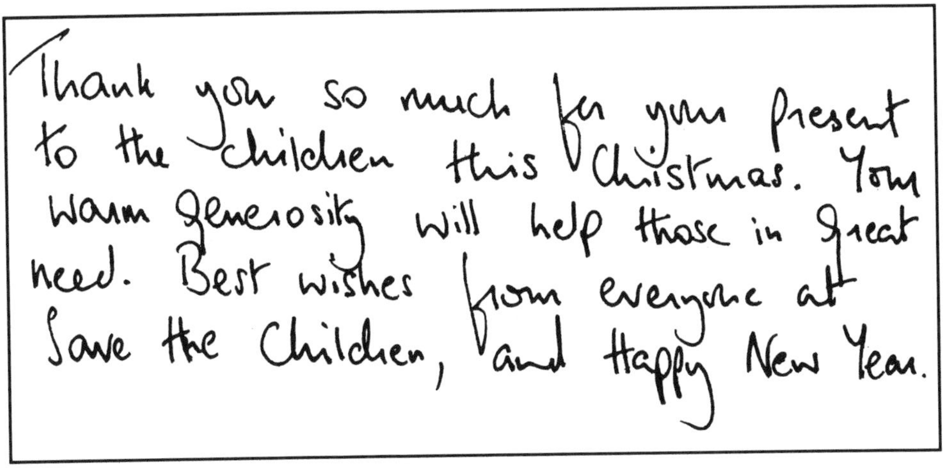
Thank you so much for your present to the children this Christmas. Your warm generosity will help those in great need. Best wishes from everyone at Save the Children, and Happy New Year.

Figure 26 Rhythmic but irregular

Rhythm can be looked at from a purely psychological point of view, attributing its cadence — Teillard likens it to the breaking of waves or the falling of leaves — to an inner state of mind, but it can also be seen as a physical function of the brain. The study of bio-rhythms suggests that there is a correct pace for all of us if we consult our own bodies instead of accepting external demands. Future graphologists may take this into account: it has links with Bunker's Graphoanalysis — based on stroke cadence — and with Dr Robert Dilts' Neuro-Linguistic Programming.

Be that as it may turn out to be, at present we accept that *writing under pressure* will disrupt the rhythm of our writing. For this reason rhythm can vary within one piece of writing, even within one word. Unconscious desires or fears, repressed because they are forbidden entry to the conscious mind rather than because we do not fulfil them, can cause sudden disruptions in the writing, and are at work behind the most seemingly rhythmic of writings (Fig. 26). Before deciding that any sample has good or lively rhythm we must be sure that it is also harmonious — without sudden, jarring irregularities or exaggerations. A second glance reveals several in Fig. 26.

Nevertheless, it has a balanced pattern of tension and release, and the writer is unlikely to be tripped up by his own unconscious impulses. We can expect to find this degree of rhythm fairly often, and — after other careful checking — may be able to say that the writer is generally well-balanced. This does not mean that all disturbed rhythm comes from the unbalanced. Check for disabilities, including a motor impulse damaged by typing.

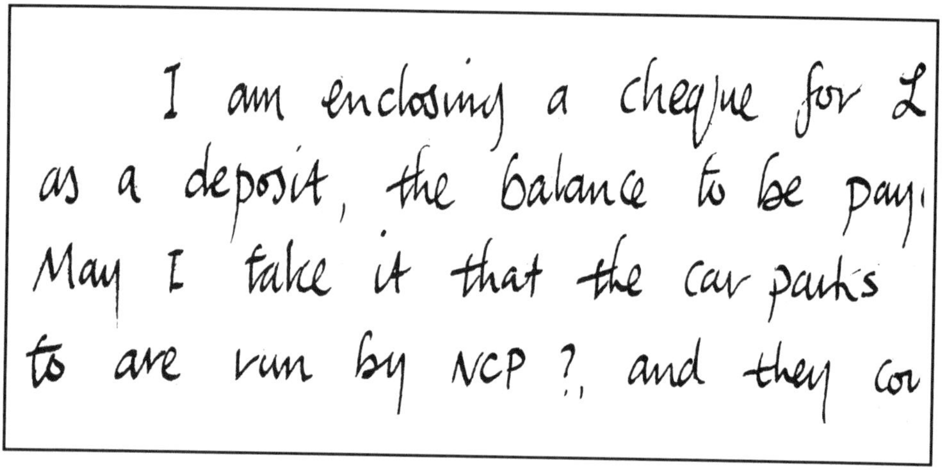

Figure 27   Rhythm stilled through effort

Much modern handwriting lacks inner rhythm, which is what elderly people mean when they refer to the low standards of writing today. Most graphologists prefer the natural expression of character found in the freer forms, knowing that mental conflict is better aired than repressed. Some decades ago, stylized forms of writing superimposed order and regularity on the natural impulses, calming disquiet and denying the inner voice. Such writers still exist, and they close the door on their unconscious mind when they turn to face the world.

Their writing may look firm and forthright, but it is largely devoid of inner rhythm. All available psychic energy is used up in effort, in maintaining a semblance of being well-balanced. Calligraphic and copybook forms often have a complete lack of rhythm — though not always — but more original writing can also show a denial of the graphic pulse. John Beck calls this *stasis* — stillness, or stilted rhythm, and many who treat the sick human mind would find it symptomizes a more negative mental state than a disturbed or uncoordinated one. When we see our neuroses we can do something about them.

Beauchataud's dry point test is helpful in defining rhythm. Do take into account immediately stressful circumstances, copying out, or physical disablement.

The Form Level

There can be no hard and fast rules about how this is assessed, since graphologists must and should use the method which best suits their own temperament. And on this point let us bear in mind the value of a full analysis of our own writing, so that we become aware of the prejudices, strengths and weaknesses with which we are investing the script before our eyes. (Psychotherapists are not licensed to practise until they have themselves undergone a course of self-analysis.) I have a theory that graphologists who write in a certain way are likely to prefer a particular method of analysis, but this is not the place to enlarge on it: it is enough to suggest that we shall not all be inclined to assess Form Level in the same way.

To some people the points system, which gives a mark between 1 (low) and 5 (high) for each of the six aspects (harmony, originality, organization, spontaneity, dynamism and rhythm) seems the fairest. The Form Level will then be represented by a total of up to thirty points. More intuitive graphologists may assess it during their first swift 'once-over', but this is a dangerously subjective way of going about it unless more specific searching is also carried out. The six aspects are each of unique importance, and within the gulf between the grading given and the possible grade of each, lies the vulnerability and fallibility of the writer. A snap judgement of high, middling or low Form Level is simply not enough. However, a careful look at each aspect, with an equally balanced overall remark as a conclusion, is equivalent to giving grades.

Before making any assessment at all, take into account external influences such as ill health, tiredness or any one of a score of factors ranging from a scratchy pen to emotional involvement in the subject of the script, temporary stress, specific damage to the arm or wrist — such as recent typing or muscle strain — and the use of lined paper. 'Making an Analysis' suggests the role of the Form Level in the final portrait.

Klages originally intended Form Level to distinguish between the mechanized and rationalized movements of the writing, and the vital impulse which indicates the creative and unique response to life of each individual. He used his High or Low Standard method of analysis to break away from the early French emphasis on signs and single features. The French later adapted Klages' innovation in the light of depth psychology, using psychoanalytical terms to describe the Formniveau, but retaining the criterion of moral superiority or inferiority imprinted in their graphology by the nineteenth century school of clerics.

Let us make our own assessments as honestly as we can, remembering that Form Level is an important aspect of graphology introduced relatively recently to Britain and America, but that it is not the whole of the subject. Clearly, for instance, it is not a form of analysis to be presented to a client! It is part of our own training and contributes to our understanding of the movement of handwriting as a whole, without finer examination.

How much psychology do we need to know in order to establish Form Level? The Abbé Michon, no less than Camillo Baldo, researched his subject before the advance of psychoanalytic theory. What he gained in careful scrutiny and comparison with the behaviour of those he met, he lost in being forced to judge by moral rather than scientifically comprehensive standards. There is value in all honest methods of graphology, providing they lead to an accurate analysis, and I believe that much depends on whose eyes the analysis is intended for. The use of psychological terms with the general public may be a waste of time or even destroy trust, but where graphology is used as a psychodiagnostic tool it is essential to have a working knowledge of current trends, and the British Institute includes some in its syllabus.

II
The Symbolic Use of Space and Direction

Overall Use of Space

The Swiss graphologist Pulver emphasized that the psychological state and intentions of the writer were etched clearly by each movement of the pen away from its starting point. If we imagine an animal with black paint on its feet leaving its hole and making its way through the world, we shall have some idea of how we, too, leave traces in our writing of our energy or our hesitancy, our willingness to leave the past and the safety of our very early childhood for the adventures and encounters of life, or our timid, spasmodic motion across a minefield of terror.

But that is not the full scope of space symbolism, for we not only reach out horizontally, but also respond to the areas above and below us. We may shrink from one of them, or we may feel more at home in one position than the other. Some people, some writers, need to keep close contact with the earth, never entirely losing touch with the solid base beneath them. Others leap from tree to tree like a squirrel, their movements light as they cover space at speed. But animal comparisons, though useful as a starting-point, must fade away when we consider the immense complexity of human behaviour in world space, or we shall meet worms with wings and leopards who never run.

Our use of the white page relates to some extent to cultural patterns and conditioning. Only in the West do we move into it from the left, progressing towards the active, productive right, and away from the inner, silent world of unexpressed knowledge, the depths of the unconscious. Semitic script travels from right to left, while Chinese and Japanese figures move in columns from top to bottom and left to right. Many graphologists believe all leftward movements in the writing to be negative, and although this term may be used in the Chinese sense of un-positive, there remains the implication that such movements are actually 'sinister' — the Latin word for left. Let us consider the table

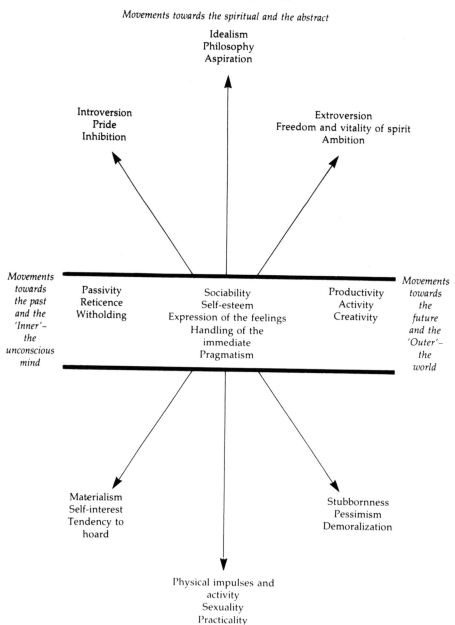

Movements towards the spiritual and the abstract

Idealism
Philosophy
Aspiration

Introversion
Pride
Inhibition

Extroversion
Freedom and vitality of spirit
Ambition

Movements towards the past and the 'Inner'– the unconscious mind

Passivity
Reticence
Witholding

Sociability
Self-esteem
Expression of the feelings
Handling of the immediate
Pragmatism

Productivity
Activity
Creativity

Movements towards the future and the 'Outer'– the world

Materialism
Self-interest
Tendency to hoard

Stubbornness
Pessimism
Demoralization

Physical impulses and activity
Sexuality
Practicality

Movements towards the real and the tangible

The Symbolic Use of Space and Direction

on page 54 in relation to the Chinese concept of Yin and Yang — the balancing movements of the T'ai Chi (Fig. 28).

Yang represents all that is light, positive, conscious and male: it symbolizes the sun, birth and the future. Yin represents all that is dark, negative, unconscious and female: it symbolizes the moon, death and the past.

These poles of light and darkness rotate, according to the concept of the Tao, and to Jung this 'circular movement has the moral significance of activating the light and dark forces of human nature, and together with them all psychological opposites of whatever kind they may be'.

Psychology and the East, p. 27

The dark Yin contains seed of the light Yang, and vice versa, so conflict is avoided and the two suggest harmonious, complementary forces.

Balance is achieved when these forces work together in mutual tolerance, without any one impulse dominating. In writing, this results in *harmony*, and leftward movements will be found in such script. Leftward tendencies are discussed further on page 87.

Figure 28 The T'ai Chi symbol of perfect balance, used by Jung in his study of the human mind.

The concept of space symbolism embraces not only the two directions of left and right, and the upper zone (above the upper bold line), middle zone and lower zone (below the lower line), but also the white spaces on the page which the ink has not covered. The links made between letters or words, and the speed and pressure with which the page surface is covered, are also part of space usage and signify aspects of the individual's adaptation to life. By shrinking some samples we can see at a glance how variable is the use of space (Fig. 29).

Margins

The subject of margins was brought into immediate focus when covering

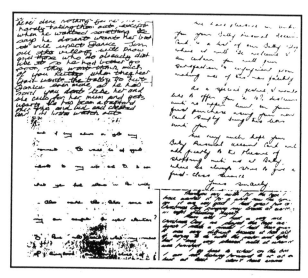

Figure 29   Use of space. The side margins are as in the original, as is the
bottom margin of the top, left hand sample.

of the page was demonstrated in Fig. 29, and this aspect of space usage
relates to the writer's opinion (conscious or unconscious) of form or
protocol.

We are taught at school how margins should be laid out, and deviation
from those rules indicates our regard or otherwise for the niceties of social
order. However, this is only true when no outside circumstances force us
to break the 'rules' of space usage, and we must be careful not to
generalize if we have to analyse only postcards — notoriously over-
covered — or notes which the writer considers private and not answerable
to scrutiny. Sometimes, too, letters are trimmed to fit envelopes, and
other paper cut for filing. The letter (bottom right) in Fig. 29 is written on
file paper, and appears to have had its left margin cut away, presumably
to get rid of the holes. The picture of space usage is therefore no longer
strictly accurate.

Graphologists give varying meanings to margin patterns, and
interpretation differs slightly according to the Form Level of the writing
and other signs. I have tried to find a common denominator for each of
the following arrangements, but it is not possible to find a general
principle behind margin layout.

(a)

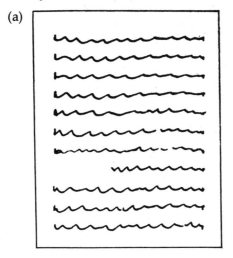

(a) Typographic margins, neat and even as book print, show a sense of form and propriety coupled with a good eye for both material (physical) and social appearances. Exact interpretation will be modified by other signs in the writing.

(b)

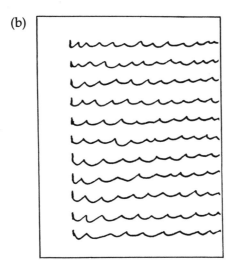

(b) Beauchataud interprets wide left margins as extroversion or generosity, and very wide ones as heedlessness (a flight from the inner to the outer). But returning to the undisputed interpretation of (a), it seems more probable that a sense of propriety or form initiates action which, once under way, stops only when circumstances force it. See also (f).

(c)

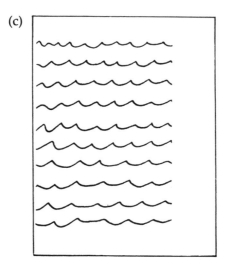

Teillard interprets wide *right* margins as heedlessness, Beauchataud as reserve or hypersensitivity, and the German school as carelessness or neglect. Again, if we return to (a), caution and conformity only set in *after* action has started: the approach of the page edge induces prudence and, depending on other signs, fear. See also (f).

(d)

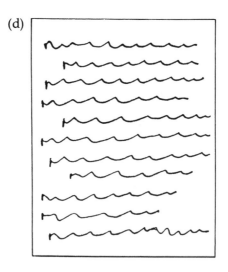

(d) Very irregular margins indicate mental abstraction from rules or form, and *must* be taken in conjunction with the Form Level and other signs. Like any other dissident behaviour they may spring from insanity, a poor planning perception, or a spontaneous and fertile mind which works from first principles rather than rules.

(e)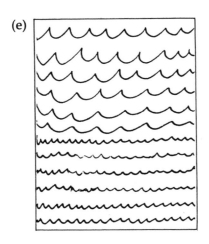

(e) Writing which covers (invades) every piece of available space — check that this is habitual and not circumstantial — shows a failure in consideration of propriety or the viewpoint of others. The whole world space in view must, it seems, be taken up in self-projection, whether this is world-conquering (large writing) or inner demanding (small writing).

(f)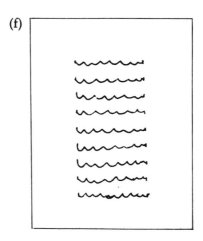

(f) The extension of (a) into exaggeratedly large margins shows fastidiousness. The writer is over-particular about the contacts he makes and the correct ordering of things. The island of world space he creates around him can also be likened to a moat, only to be crossed by using the correct password.

(g)
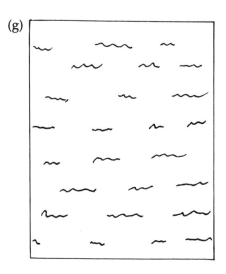

(g) A need for solitude and space, unrelated to propriety or social discrimination — see (f) — is found here. See the bottom left sample in Fig. 29.

All assessments of margins need to be based on the agreed interpretation of (a). Complex formations such as increasing or decreasing margins should be interpreted in its light.

Word-Spacing

The last margin example (g) brought the space between words into focus.

Wide spacing (wider than two letter widths) shows a *deliberate distancing from other people*, although the reason for this will be indicated by other signs. In good Form Level writing it probably shows self-sufficiency and ample mental resources, but in other script it may indicate rough treatment from others and ensuing distrust, or a feeling of being unable to relate socially.

Such writing gives the impression of word-islands set in large areas of open space. The writer may appear cold and aloof, even isolated in his

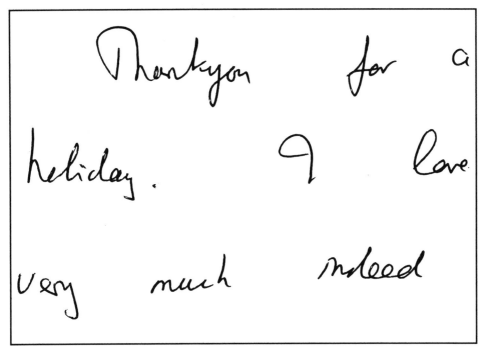

Figure 30   Wide word spacing

reserve: if he does not, take note of his need for solitude or you may suddenly find yourself shut out, the doors to his mind apparently slammed in your face.

Narrow spacing between words (less than one letter width) is significant to the graphologist but also needs to be noted in personal encounters. Sometimes, but not always, it features in lean, concentrated writing (see Fig. 39), and is sometimes accompanied by extreme closeness of the lines of writing.

Lack of space between words shows a *need for human contact*, and may also indicate the easy, blunt manner which so often typifies those who love a crowd. Such writers may cling to those they hold dear, and also to their possessions, since there is some insecurity in the need to be surrounded by others. Other signs in the writing may indicate as much hostility, frustration and fear of others as in widely spaced script. All we learn from spacing is the writer's *preference*: the reasons for it may be subtle.

Regular word-spacing would seem to show a calm social attitude which seeks neither isolation nor constant shoulder-rubbing, but we must be

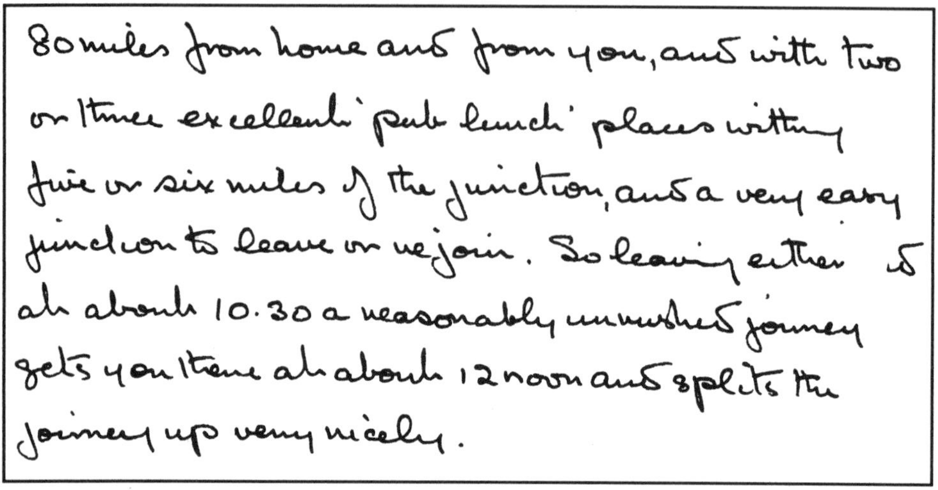

80 miles from home and from you, and with two
or three excellent 'pub lunch' places within
five or six miles of the junction, and a very easy
junction to leave or rejoin. So leaving either
at about 10.30 a reasonably unrushed journey
gets you there at about 12 noon and splits the
journey up very nicely.

Figure 31 Narrow word spacing

I shall really be looking for
to going home on Thurs
after a day's Shopping

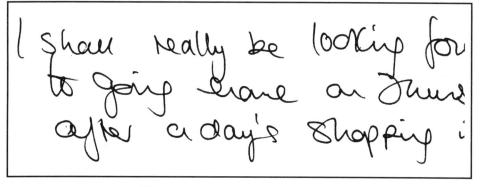

Figure 32 Irregular word spacing

careful about making this judgement. Maintaining one's own world space does not exclude a multitude of bitter feelings towards our fellow men, and calligraphic writing, showing a nature which seeks an ideal, is an unreliable guide in this respect. So is copybook writing, with its desire to conform to the standards of others. *Regular* spacing cannot be a *dominant* in writing.

Irregular spacing, on the other hand, where a long gap between words is followed by a narrow space, shows an irregular need of company and such a person may confuse his neighbours by unpredictable moods or withdrawal into solitude. Variations in word-spacing are not always great, but measuring can show frequent minor discrepancies. This aspect of graphology is covered under 'Regularity' on page 143. Words linked by a stroke are discussed on page 76.

Dimension (Size)

This aspect of space usage is also subject to controversy, partly because insufficient attention is paid to the need to adapt the size of one's writing to circumstance. The size of the signature is a different matter and is discussed much later.

However, it is important to have some guideline on what *is* big writing, or how small it must be to be called 'small'. Measurement is taken from the middle zone only, that part of the writing which lies between the two lines as shown on page 93.

Normal or average dimension means that the middle zone of the writing is between $1\frac{1}{2}$ and $2\frac{1}{2}$ mm high. Writing which is habitually of average size can only indicate that a balance is achieved between the qualities attributed to large or small writing.

Large writing. Handwriting is classified as large if the central zone is more than $2\frac{1}{2}$ mm in height.

The reason for this exaggerated size is closely tied to other facets of the writing, and we need to be sure that such size is habitual before making any assessment at all.

The overall significance of large writing, taking the views of French and German graphologists into account, is that the writer *needs or demands space to project himself.* Impulses stemming from pride, vanity,

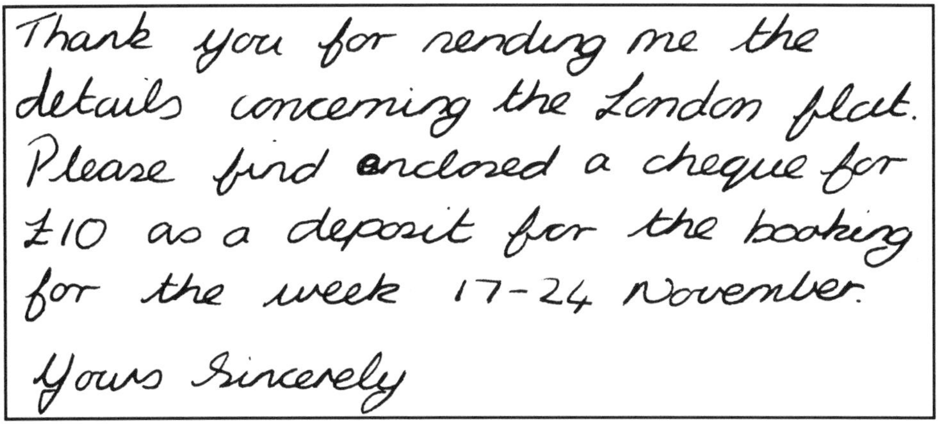

Thank you for sending me the details concerning the London flat. Please find enclosed a cheque for £10 as a deposit for the booking for the week 17–24 November.

Yours Sincerely

Figure 33 Average dimension ($1\frac{1}{2}$–$2\frac{1}{2}$ mm)

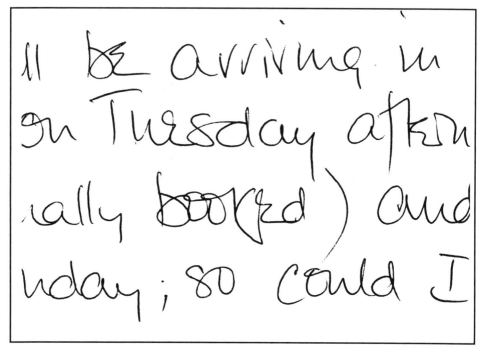

Figure 34   Large writing (more than 2½ mm)

enthusiasm, dynamism, strong feelings or vigorous activity may cause this need, and we can make no specific assessment until the rest of the writing has been examined. The writing above shows originality, dynamism, organization and spontaneity and some rhythm: we can also note small but definite margins and average/narrow word spaces. Here is an excess of vitality well projected, but not all large writing shows so many positive qualities.

Small writing. Handwriting is classified as small if the central zone is less than 1½ mm in height.

The reason for this exaggeratedly small dimension is related to other aspects of the writing, and we need to be sure that the writer is not just adapting to a small space.

We shall find later that the dimension of the middle zone corresponds to the writer's concept of himself, and generally speaking a small middle zone indicates modesty and a limited need of world space for self-expression. This is sometimes, but by no means always, linked to a capacity for patient, precise research and penetrating thinking. Where the Form Level is poor, lack of confidence or any kind of personal fulfilment is indicated, but where the style is organized copybook, a pernickety nature may find satisfaction in fine close-work. Accuracy and concentration will be corroborated by other signs in the writing, and the self-image is almost always established by the signature.

The sample in Fig. 35 shows a proud, private nature which paints life with intricate, painstaking strokes on a small canvas. Double-checking takes the place of originality or dynamism.

Decreasing dimension. Though graphologists differ in precise interpretation, all seem to agree that words which decrease in size show a *withdrawal from exteriorization*. Thoughts and feelings are not completely projected or expressed due to a lack of final impulse, and this negativity may be difficult to assess.

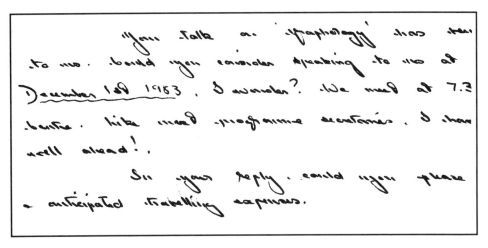

Figure 35 Small writing (less than 1½ mm)

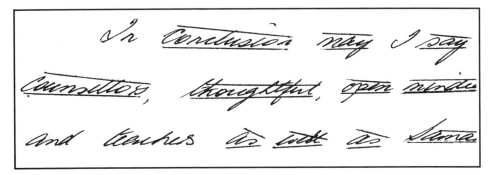

Figure 36 Decreasing dimension

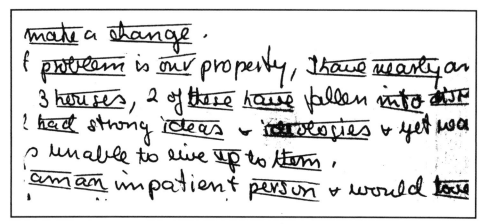

Figure 37   Increasing dimension

Impatience, haste or pressure of work are suggested in good Form Level writing, especially since this formation is so often accompanied by signs of debility. But in firm, organized writing which lacks originality or spontaneity, Michon's definition of subtlety and cunning may apply. The German school finds diplomacy in decreasing size — a good Form Level version of the above. The middle zone drops from 5 mm to 1 mm at times in Fig. 36.

Increasing dimension. This shows an *increase in exteriorization*: increased effort, candour and emphasis. Such ardent, artless projection may suggest childishness, and certainly the writer lacks subtlety and subterfuge. I think of this formation as 'the trumpet'.

Horizontal Tension

In discussing the use of page or world space, it is interesting to note restriction or otherwise in the movement from left to right. This tension in the writing causes letter forms to vary, and we have already seen that word spacing is affected by the ease with which the writer advances across space or fears the isolation of such a move.

Form

Spaced out letters
The width of the middle zone letters in relation to their height shows whether the words are advancing eagerly across the page, or hugging their position. For the moment we are disregarding word spacing.

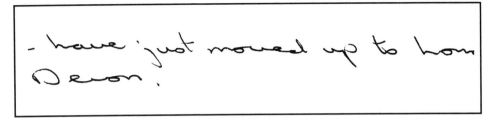

Figure 38 Spaced out writing

When the letters are wider than they are high, we say that the writing is spaced out. This forward-reaching movement shows that the nature is being exteriorized with little reserve or restriction. It is released writing, with minimal tension or withholding. Such writing can indicate *natural self-expression in the social sphere, frankness, generosity or sheer dissipation,* and in high Form Level writing a need to project the self outwards through creativity.

In the sample shown in Fig. 38, interpretation will have to be modified by the left slant of the writing — another warning that all assessments must be taken in conjunction with one another.

Lean writing
Writing whose middle zone letters are higher than they are wide is known as lean writing (Fig. 39).

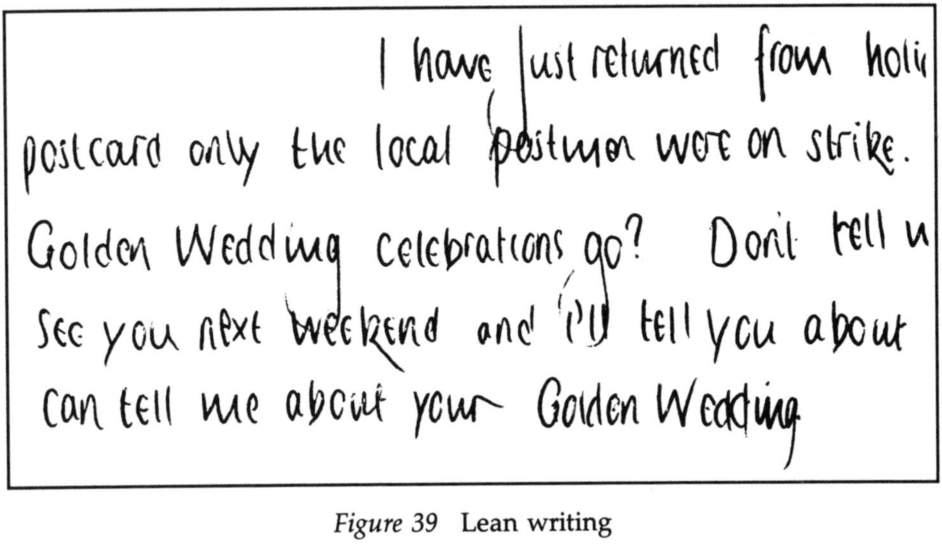

I have just returned from holi
postcard only the local postman were on strike.
Golden Wedding celebrations go? Don't tell u
See you next weekend and I'll tell you about
can tell me about your Golden Wedding

Figure 39 Lean writing

Here the writing is restricted, held back by horizontal tension as the hand moves reluctantly across the page. Such restricted movement may be reflected in the expressiveness of the whole body.

This reining-back of the nature is *a form of withholding*, and for this reason some graphologists link other kinds of meanness with lean writing. Yet very often the rest of the writing shows this to be unlikely, and that instead a fundamental prudence and caution governs the mind. This may include a gift for abstract thinking, concentrating on essential facts whilst automatically controlling the feelings and the imagination. Large, lean writing makes the withholding urge a personal virtue.

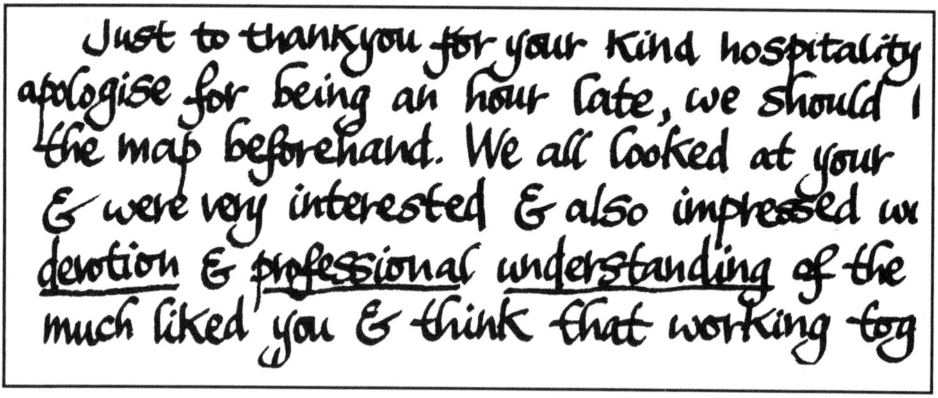
Just to thankyou for your kind hospitality
apologise for being an hour late, we should l
the map beforehand. We all looked at your
& were very interested & also impressed wi
devotion & professional understanding of the
much liked you & think that working tog

Figure 40 Concentrated writing

So we see that this withheld, restricted aspect of the writing is but a part of the jigsaw, and can have no precise interpretation without being taken in conjunction with neighbouring pieces. The lack of harmony and rhythm in the writing in Fig. 39 suggests considerable conflict of spirit — in itself a deterrent to the free and spontaneous embracing of life.

Concentrated writing

When lean writing combines with narrow word-spacing and close lines, the effect is an imbalance of black against white: space is crowded by concentrated writing. Postcards often show a deliberate packing-down and packing-in of words, but this is not at all comparable to writing which is unnecessarily concentrated into a small space on a large sheet of paper.

Such writing shows *intense and immediate involvement*. Again, we must consider the Form Level before assessing it, because whilst one writer remains attached to the present and to his immediate surroundings through an instinct to gossip and control events — to dominate his environment — another puts his need for instant self-expression into creative literary or oratory work. Yet another is impelled towards disciplined, precise work, and shows a narrow-minded lack of vision. Thus the tension, the sense of immediacy and reality of the concentrated writer must be judiciously interpreted, even when it is habitual.

Once in a while, a love of economy to the point of meanness is a justifiable assessment, but this graphological old wives' tale must only occasionally contribute its grain of truth.

Concentrated words in isolation

A sudden contraction of the wrist, caused by a swift withholding impulse in the mind, can produce isolated groups of concentrated words in otherwise spaced-out writing.

These show *intense, immediate involvement of a negative kind* — like a snail or a tortoise sharply withdrawing its head. The word or words involved usually give a clue in themselves as to the source of grievance, but we also find markedly concentrated formations in signatures. Patches of concentrated writing indicate close attention to the subject in hand, and sometimes a fear that space will run out before all has been said.

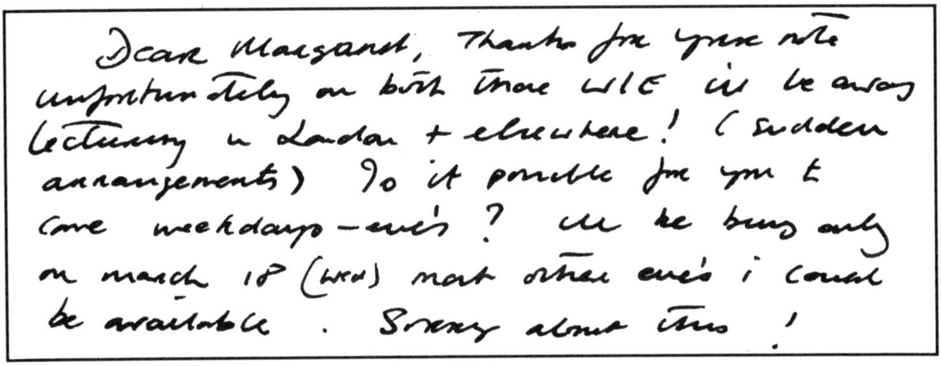
Dear Margaret, Thanks for your note
unfortunately on both those W/E I'll be away
lecturing in London + elsewhere! (sudden
arrangements) Is it possible for you to
come weekdays-eve's? I'll be busy only
on March 18 (Wed) most other eve's I could
be available. Sorry about this!

Figure 41 Isolated concentrated words (top two lines)

Sometimes the writer slows down to check the spelling of a word, and this may result in a spasm of concentration which disrupts the rhythm.

These points show how careful we must be in assessing concentrated writing. In the sample shown in Fig. 41, the writing moves from concentration in the first lines to a more natural (given the letter width) aerated form. (See also Fig. 1).

Aerated writing

When spaced-out writing combines with sufficient word-spacing and

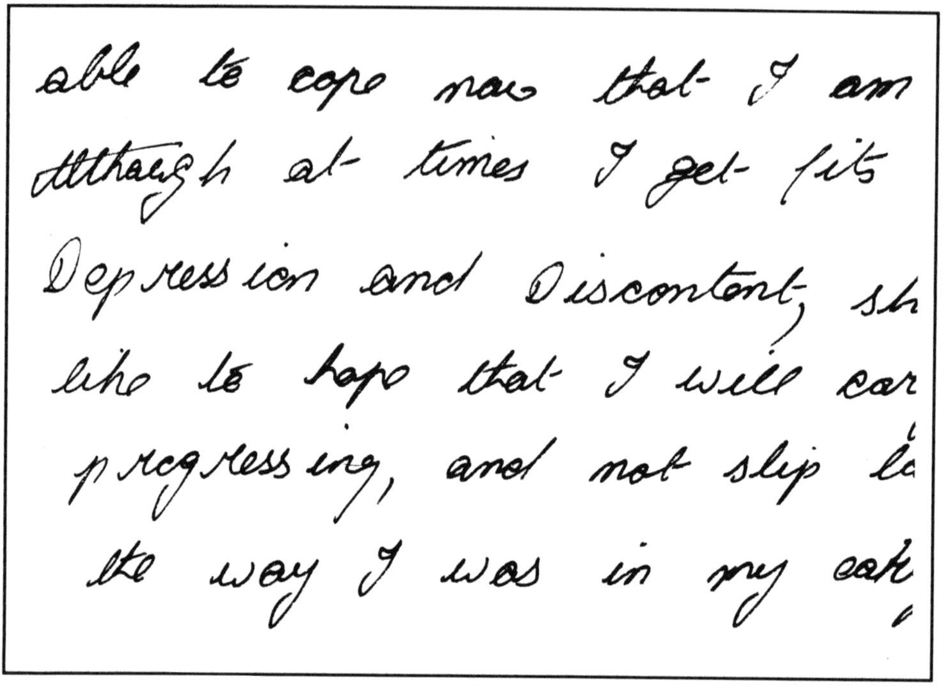

Figure 42 Aerated writing

adequately separated lines, the writing is known as **aerated**. This is generally taken to indicate *an ability to take a detached, objective view* in contrast to the close involvement shown in concentrated writing. A balanced, though not excessive, interspersing of the writing by white space, shows detached and independent judgement — the ability to stand back a little in order to see more clearly.

It follows that this wider view may sometimes lack the precision of closely involved application; that the writer may sometimes wander from the point or move on a little too quickly. Once more the Form Level is likely to help in interpretation, and other signs in the writing will also have a bearing on it.

Aerated words in isolation
A sudden release within the mind can produce a word or group of words which appear as an aerated island in a sea of concentrated writing. These mark a *lifting of the spirits away* from the particular and the present, towards future, hope or aspiration. Usually, the words themselves spell

out the cause of such a forward surge, and frequently they will be names or places.

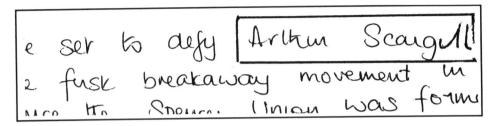

Figure 43   Isolated aerated words

Such isolated patches of productive and progressive impulsion show that the individual has the capacity to live that way if he chooses. It can be therapeutic to pick out the causes of that impulse, and to nurture them, just as it is wise to take note of the reasons for concentration (contraction) in the writing.

Slant
There is general agreement amongst graphologists on this aspect of handwriting, though French schools put greater emphasis on its emotional significance, while German and Swiss tend to assess it in terms of sociability. We are talking about the angle of the script: its inclination towards the left (backslant), the right (forward slant) or its lack of inclination at all (upright).

Space symbolism suggests a physical move towards or away from world space, or a maintaining position uninfluenced by pressure from in front or behind.

Upright writing
Though modified by other signs and by the quality of its Form Level, this signifies *independence of spirit* — a standing on one's own two feet. It is sensible to lay a pencil along the upright strokes to make sure that the writing is actually upright, and not at a slight angle, and also that the slant is habitual. In Fig. 44 a few uprights slant slightly leftwards, but the writing remains basically upright for five large pages.

Depending on other aspects, upright writing can indicate stability, indifference, firmness or strong will, self-control, coldness, pride, reserve, rigidity, individuality or prudence.

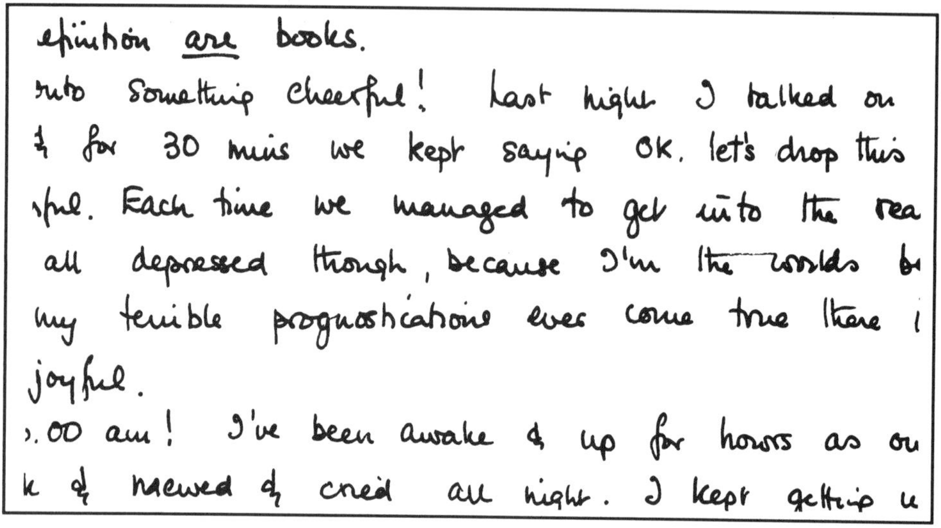

efinition are books.
nto Something cheerful! Last night I talked on
& for 30 mins we kept saying OK. let's drop this
yful. Each time we managed to get into the rea
all depressed though, because I'm the worlds b
my terrible prognostications ever come true there i
joyful.
..00 am! I've been awake & up for hours as ou
k & mewed & cried all night. I kept getting u

Figure 44 Upright writing

Right slant

This symbolizes *a movement to greet the world*; imagine a human figure with arms outstretched. Depending on the angle, imagine the figure making a slight or an expansive gesture in a forward direction. Such habitual writers are chiefly concerned with what they are going to do to the world:

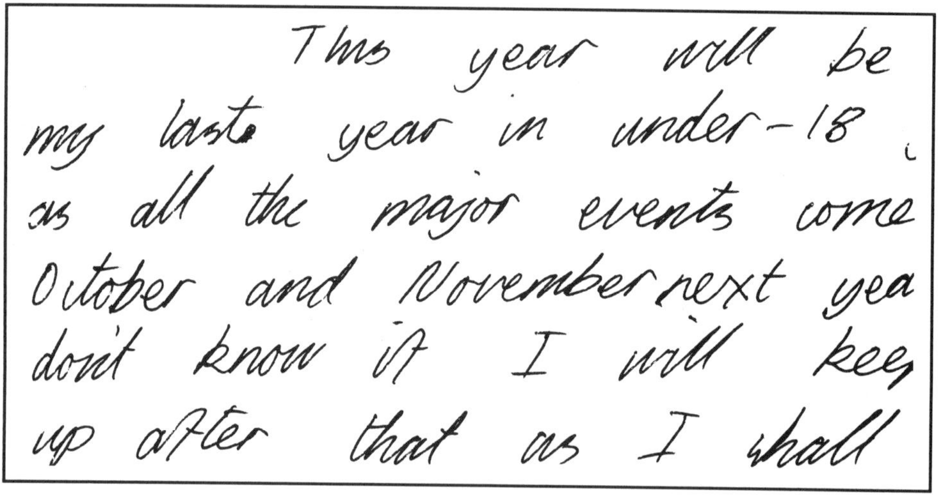

This year will be
my last year in under-18 ,
as all the major events come
October and November next yea
don't know if I will kee,
up after that as I shall

Figure 45 Right (forward) slant

they fight actively to reach their goals, and interact strongly with whatever situation faces them.

This attitude is generally termed extrovert, but in practice this is far too general a description. Very light writing, for instance, shows impressionability and sensitivity. Though socially aware and often seeking approval or status, other signs may indicate rigidity or earthiness, domination or implacable self-will. In good Form Level writing we may discover a creative spirit fired to help mankind.

The writing in Fig. 45 lacks rhythm and harmony and is not particularly sociable. Its slant suggests a systematic assault on life,but there are other signs, to be recognized later.

Left (back) slant

If those whose writing slants forward are generally preoccupied by what they are going to do to the world, left or back-slanters are chiefly concerned about what the world is going to do to them.

A left slant does not feature in copybook or calligraphic teaching, therefore its adoption represents, however unconsciously, *a rebellion or a refusal in the face of life*. Imagine a human figure leaning backwards, its stance *varying from a slight withdrawal to a ready-to-run abhorrence* of what it sees before it. With this as our only fundamental assessment, let us remember the transforming power of a good Form Level, and the significance of other dominant signs in the writing.

The French, basing their judgement on the moral superiority of Michon

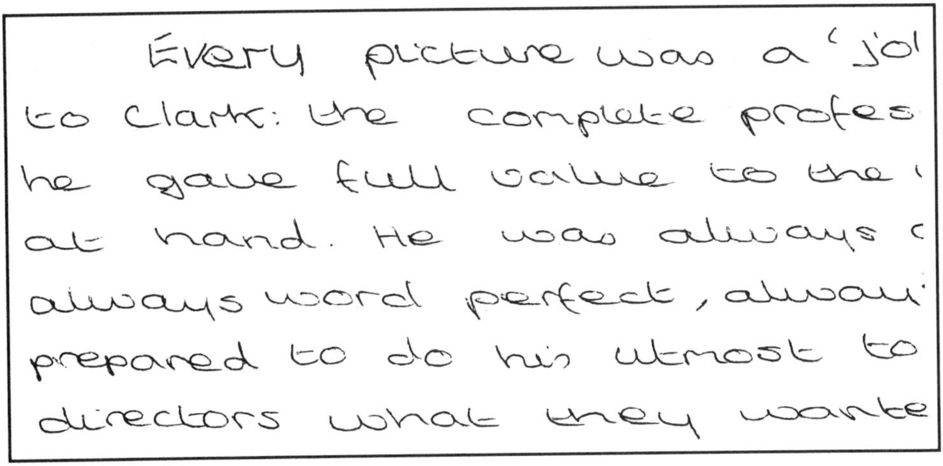

Figure 46 Left (back) slant

and Crepieux-Jamin, have nothing good to say about a left slant. The Germans see it as a psychological retreat into the past, and may depict the writer as still living out his childhood, withdrawing into his own secret paradise in an elusive, sideways encounter with the world. Negativity, fear, distrust or hypersensitivity may produce a left slant, but we must be careful not to consider our Western standards as an absolute truth. Let us remember that half the world faces back to the womb and the dark for preference, and they may know better than we do.

If we cannot understand, let us be compassionate without understanding.

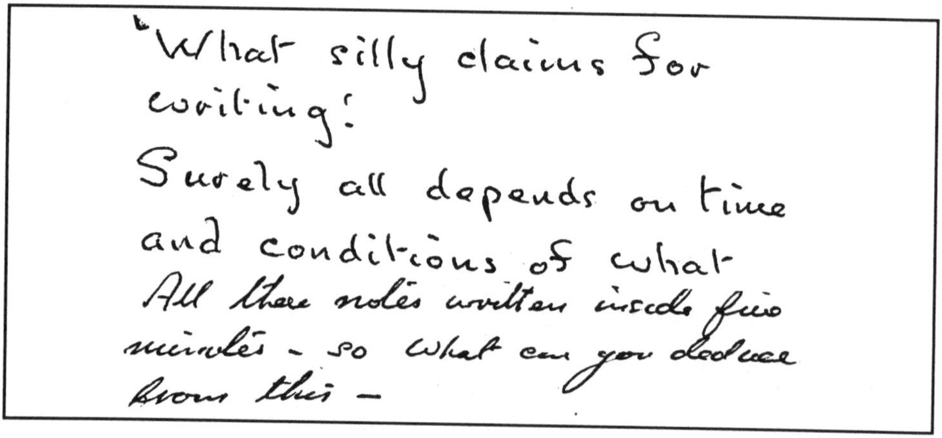

Figure 47 Mixed slant

Mixed slant
This occurs when a writer habitually adopts varying slants according to what he is writing. Some people, through strongly subjective feelings, readjust to differing circumstances, sometimes making great efforts of adaptation. Others can reorientate themselves at will, like an actor changing roles.

We must pay more attention if a complete change of orientation to the world has taken place. I often ask if the left slant is a new development: if so, it is flight or refusal based on bad experience.

Irregular slant
This shows emotional and social disturbance (often temporary); an inner conflict between advancing, retreating or enduring. Indecision and mixed feelings make it difficult for the writer to adjust to the demands of life, and he may be very unhappy.

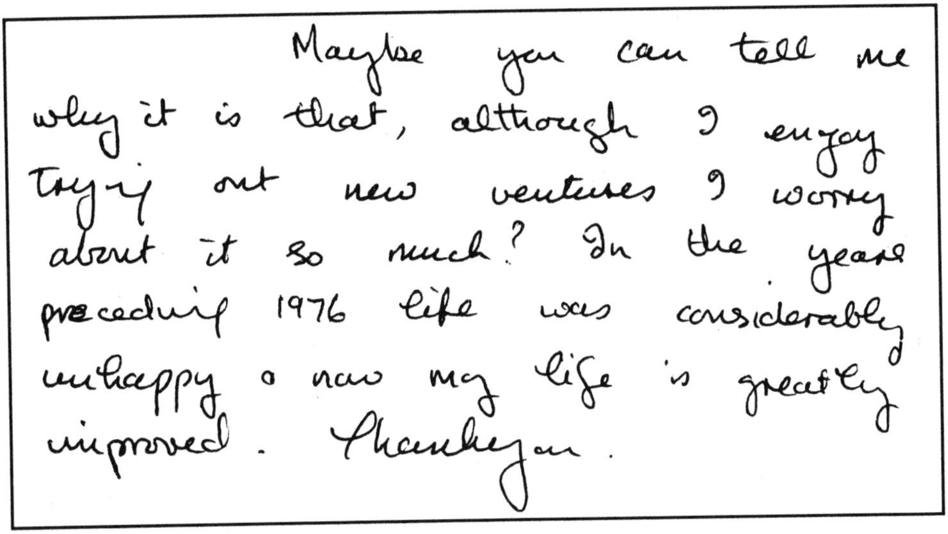

Figure 48   Irregular slant

Continuity

Letters are put together to form words, and the way in which we link them up to make progress across the page represents another form of horizontal tension.

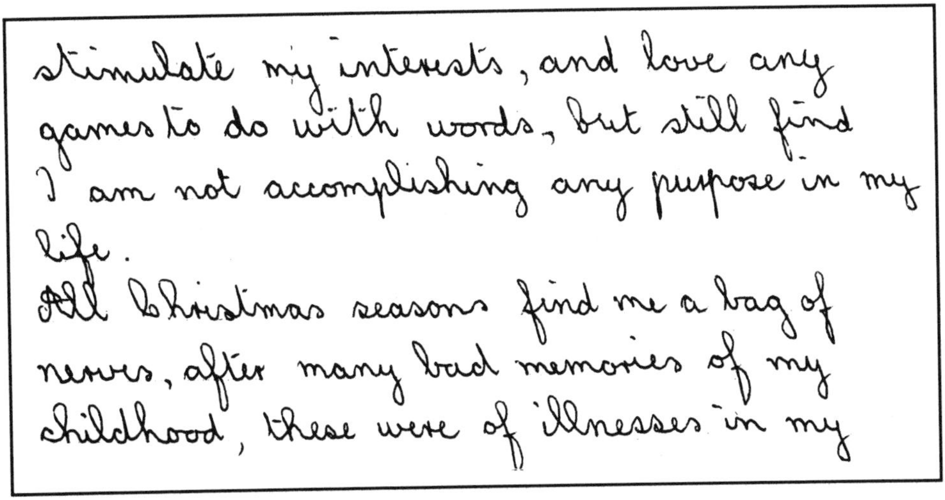

Figure 49   Strongly connected

In this country we are all taught at some stage to join up our letters. We may find this easy, but we may also find that, try as we will, breaks appear between the letters of our writing. It seems that the continuity of our writing is tied to a natural rhythm in our minds, and it is difficult to alter this pattern in our script.

Linked writing

Linked writing (whole words or more than five letters together) shows *a rational and realistic following-through of ideas,* and it is hard to deflect such a writer from the course of his thoughts and efforts. In poor Form Level writing it indicates routine activity and lack of initiative, but in high Form Level logical, deductive and systematic thought processes are likely.

Hyper-linked writing

This kind of writing, in which whole sentences may be joined together, shows single-mindedness taken to the point of bigotry or even fanaticism. The connection is forced, showing *a lack of attunement to changing world conditions.* This remains true when linked words feature in fairly disconnected writing, although here outstanding gifts for logical combination or scientific research exist. See Figs. 5 and 14.

Partly connected writing

Very large numbers of people link two or three letters before lifting their

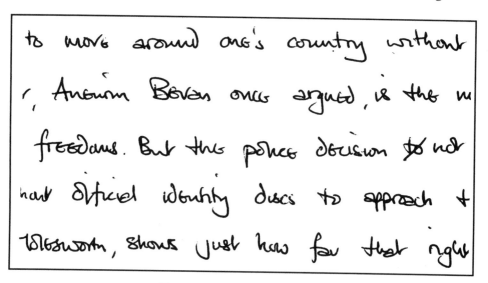

Figure 50   Partly connected

pen and restarting to write, and this may produce a unified appearance and some rhythm in the writing. I see this movement as that of an aware animal, moving across world space in a continuous movement, but stopping very briefly to lift its head and check what is happening around it.

All graphologists see such continuity as a mark of *adaptability of thought*, and of good co-ordination between ideas and acts. In high Form Level script, critical observation or an inventive spirit may be indicated, but in all writing where the forward movement is organized and uninhibited, there is a degree of intuition at work amid the mind's logical, systematic flow.

Partly connected writing does not include script of **mixed connection**, often with large gaps in the centre of words. This is described on page 78.

Disconnected writing (all letters separate)
There are *two kinds of disconnected writing*, and they are quite easy to distinguish.

The traditional interpretation of a tendency to isolate all things without seeing them as part of a pattern — being 'unable to see the wood for the trees' — needs modifying. It is true that in very poor Form Level writing, or where the letters have become disconnected through age or debility (disorganized), there may be a lack of logic and co-ordination, but in light, aerated writing, *abundant intuition* may combine with a fine intellect. Abbé Michon's assessment of intuition is rarely acknowledged by the French, but Fig. 51 shows the form in which it appears.

In heavy, typographic script, *a sense of visual order* is shown, and this may dominate logical thinking processes. An insistence on certain methods of presentation may make the writer seem selfish or egocentric, but often he is gifted.

To some extent I know that I stand alone in appreciating the gifts shown in disconnected writing. Self-expression of an eccentric nature may be linked with it — such writers avoid lined paper — and are probably impelled by logic other than that of intellectual discipline. Nevertheless, interpretation should be less negative and more aware than it often is.

Capitals throughout
This is an artificial form of disconnection, and is caused mainly by *anxiety* and a strong desire to be understood. The self-expression produced by the writer's normal script dissatisfies him, so there is an element of shame or frustration. Other interpretations are speculative.

winding silent
yawn to van
mystery

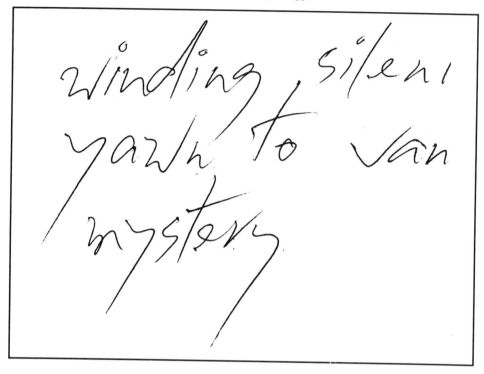

Figure 51 Disconnected (intuitive)

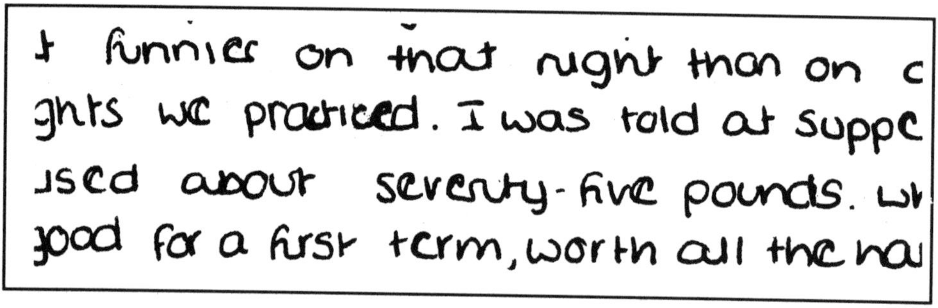

t funnier on that night than on c
ghts we practiced. I was told at suppe
used about seventy-five pounds. wh
good for a first term, worth all the ha

Figure 52 Disconnected (visual)

Mixed connection

This is generally the result of *frustration and overstrain of the mind*: the writer finds it hard to equate the facts he is trying to assimilate, and the difficulty may be temporary. Where there are large gaps in words he may

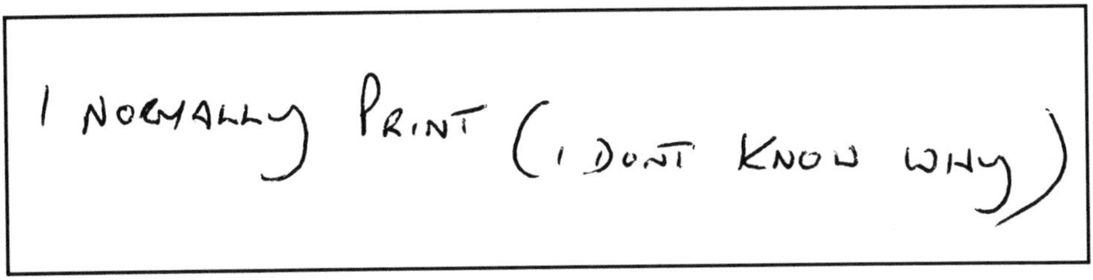

Figure 53 Capitals throughout

be close to mental breakdown. He may need a change of job, but in low Form Level writing the problem may be habitual.

Form of connection

The way in which letters are joined together (connected) takes us back to our symbolic first steps into world space. Remembering that in our culture we write from left to right, imagine once more an animal leaving its hole and advancing towards the future and the right: its footsteps can be compared with forms of connection.

Every time one of our feet hits the ground we make a forward move, and these forward moves are represented in writing by strokes. The way the pen moves upwards and forwards in order to make another downstroke is significant, and describes our manner walking into and across our lives.

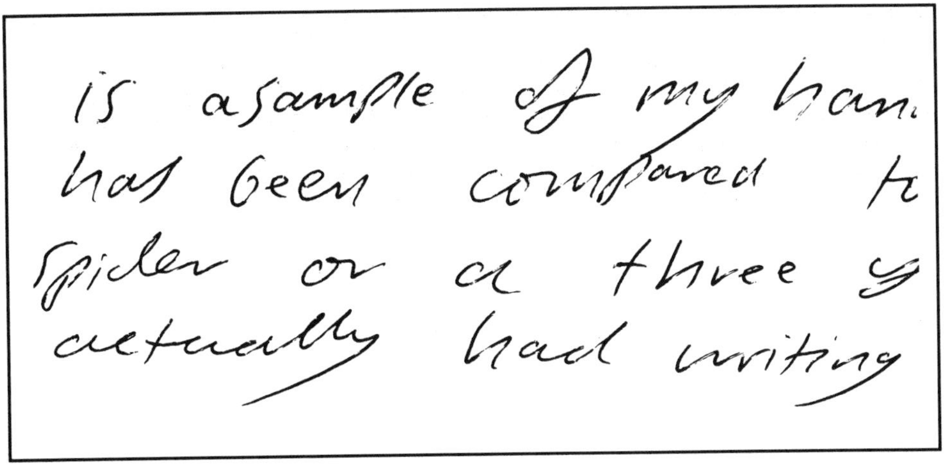

Figure 54 Mixed connection

Angular writing

Here the writer marches, his rigid pace leaving no room for nuances of feeling of circumstances. *Such a writer deals in facts,* and he tends to live by these: thus he is probably loyal and reliable but with a certain lack of flexibility. Much depends on the Form Level, for with other signs of stubbornness or strong will, the negative aspect of this masculine trait will be pronounced, whilst light pressure (page 126), originality and spontaneity add a creative dimension.

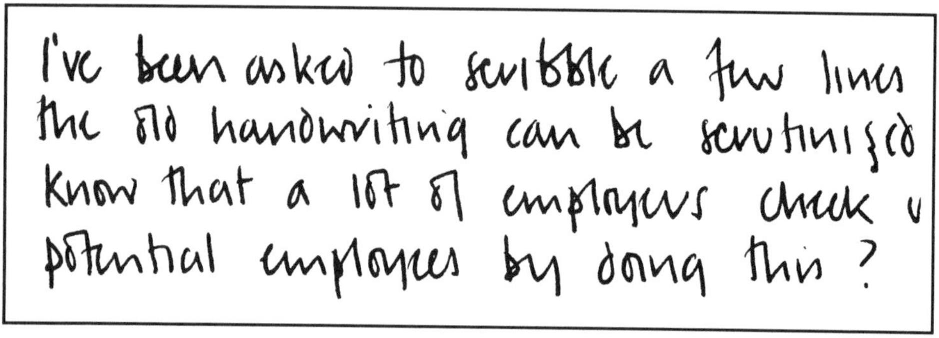

I've been asked to scribble a few lines
the old handwriting can be scrutinised
know that a lot of employers check v
potential employees by doing this ?

Figure 55 Angular form of connection

Rounded forms of connection

Roundness in writing signifies an interplay of the feelings on life events. (In Fig. 55, roundness was eliminated to the greatest extent possible.) In likening form of connection to gait, we must think of our animal making progress with a smooth tread, *absorbing the unevenness in the ground* as he takes care how he goes. This does not imply a slow, but a more adaptable pace.

Garland connection

Here the rounded movements are concave and stay close to the earth. The writer glides along with an easy-going acceptance ranging from supple and rapid assessment (small writing) to passive indifference (soft or feeble writing). Between these lie many patterns of concerned and sentimental behaviour, but all have in common the low base of earthiness: garland connections are not a sign of spiritual or uplifted feeling, but of practical and pragmatic adaptability.

Very rapid garland connections lose their depth of feeling: here the chief object is the end in view, and the writer 'runs' towards it. This is

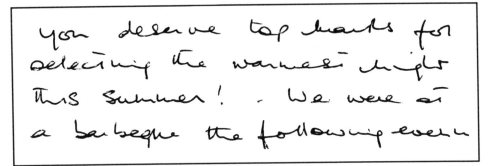

Figure 56 Garland form of connection

what happens when we rush our notes; all caring is concentrated on the end product — getting there.

Arcade connection
This subtle and slightly disputed way of moving forward requires greater effort than the garland, and is less relaxed. Its continual arching can be likened to walking on tiptoe in a more or less calculated attitude.

Why not walk on tiptoe? Depending on Form Level and spontaneity, we shall find that the 'uplift' is due to one or more of the following: a dislike of earthy vulgarity; snobbery (highly organized or calligraphic writing); artistic or aesthetic sense; screening of the thoughts to create an improved image; a lofty, haughty outlook bred from birth and therefore unconscious; or, in poor Form Level writing, the habitually flattering attitude of a 'creep'.

Mixed form of connection (snaking or wavy line)
Sometimes garland and arcade forms combine in alternate patterns, twisting and snaking in what is indeed a flexible, diplomatic but manipulative movement. Such a writer makes careful use of outside circumstances and conditions, and adapts his feelings to them.

Thread connection
This movement covers page and ground fast, and that is its main aim. The writer's mind is on the future rather than the present, so there may be a lack of awareness of the nuances of the moment — and perhaps a skirting of any potential holdups — as he sprints towards his goal. Thread writers dislike wasting time, and many of life's more lofty or profound areas of concern are put into the category of time-wasting, which is why such script tends to remain on one intermediate level. Words whose endings

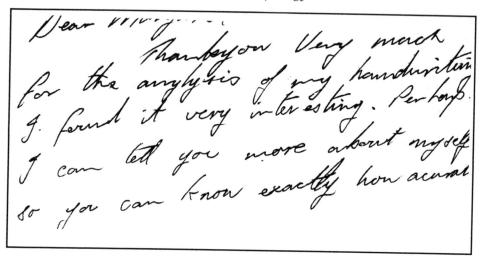

Figure 57   Arcade connection

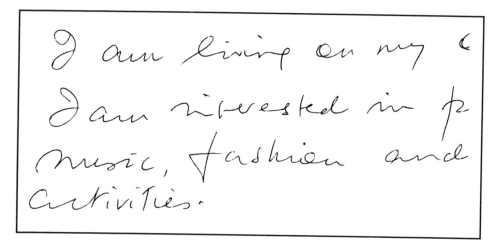

Figure 58   Mixed, wavy line connection

only turn into a thread are indicative of an impatient but intelligent mind which constantly recalls itself to present awareness. See also Fig. 15.

Copybook connection

When the writing shows no distinctive method of connection — no errant curves or marked patterns of linking — and providing it is linked at all, it

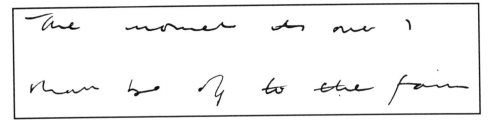

Figure 59 Thread connection

may be following the form the writer was taught. If so, a tendency to conform is shown: the writer wants to follow an approved path through life, and so he walks correctly and carefully across world space. He attaches value to convention, despite other signs which might seem to deny this.

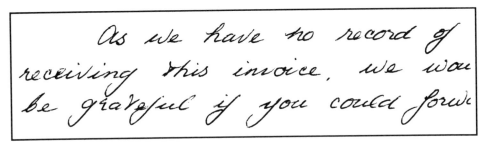

Figure 60 Copybook connection

Speed

We are still considering horizontal tension — the way in which the individual progresses across world space from his starting-point on the left. The *manner* in which he moves, shown symbolically by the writing in its spacing, dimension, concentration, slant, continuity and form of connection, is quite different from the *speed* at which he moves. *Only thread connection has speed as its dominating characteristic*: the other movements we have looked at are in essence psychological approaches to life.

Speed is facilitated when the writing is an automatic response to what is in the mind, and not a conscious and laboured process. An awareness of pen movement, or anxiety about the final appearance of the script, will slow its pace and destroy its spontaneity, organization and rhythm, which is why graphologists cannot assess fairly those samples which have been created for their eyes. The writing in Fig. 61 contains signs associated with speed but is actually slow, and the artificially disconnected script of Fig. 62 is slow/calm, not the writer's natural pace.

Slow writing
Slow script (fewer than 100 letters per minute) shows *a degree of calculation during its production*, but we must look at other aspects of the writing to decide why this should be so. Perhaps the writer is uneducated, or using a formation alien to his own culture (as probably in Fig. 62), but he may also be deliberately disguising his writing. The slowing effects of this can be a key factor in identifying forgeries. In these cases the Form Level will be poor.

But in good Form Level writing, slowness may indicate courtesy and reserve, self-discipline and deep reflective thought. Generally, a passive character is suggested, but slow, heavy writing indicates stubbornness or intransigence — the habitual digging-in of heels.

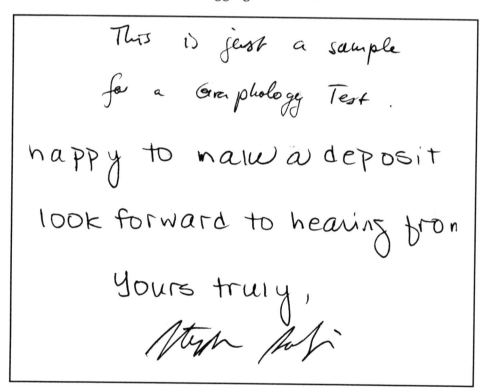

Figures 61 and 62   Artificially slow

Naturally slow writing can be recognized by these signs:

rounded formation

thick, heavy strokes

decreasing left margin

disconnected writing (in poor Form Level)

increasing dimension

painstaking detail

decorations and flourishes

retouching of strokes

Speed can be assessed quite well by the use of a dry point and a stopwatch, but this is not necessary except in special cases. Dry-point tests are chiefly used to find inhibited or contraflow movements, and when the writing appears to have a stop/start, mixed speed action (see Figs. 37 and 112) there is a frustrated desire for action and self-expression, similar to mixed connection (see Fig. 54). Do take into account justified causes for this, such as embarrassing subject matter, a struggle with spelling or a foreign language, problems with composition or continual interruptions. Remember to check that the formation is habitual.

Figure 63   Slow (fewer than 100 l.p.m.)

Calm writing

This regular pace — around 130 letters per minute — shows a calm and purposeful progression in good Form Level writing, but caution and prudence taken to the point of intractability in very heavy or low Form Level script. Very soft or light writing shows submission. Calm writing is usually well-organized, without hasty movements or much spontaneity.

As the speed of the writing increases, regularity decreases, since it is difficult to perfect precise details at speed. The writing begins to show simplified strokes and short cuts, and there is less variation in stroke direction.

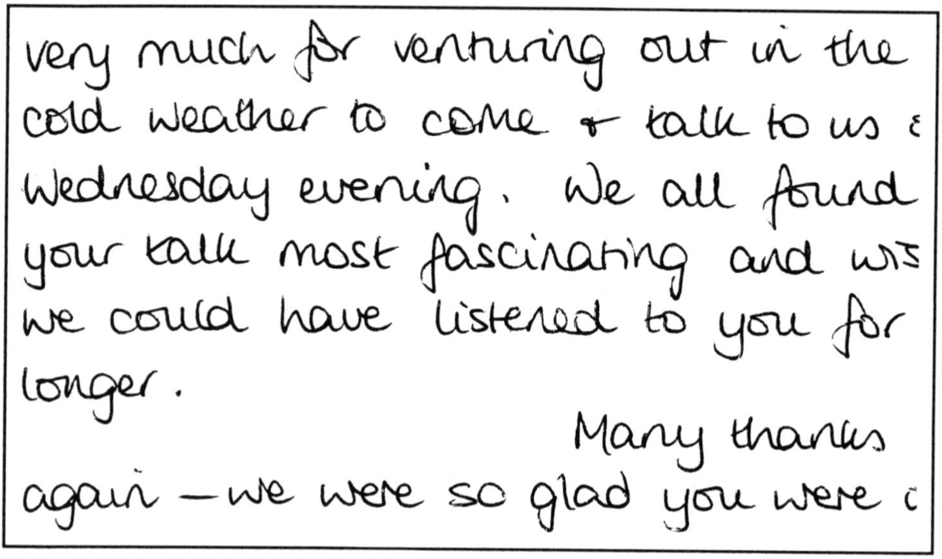

> very much for venturing out in the
> cold weather to come + talk to us ε
> Wednesday evening. We all found
> your talk most fascinating and wis
> we could have listened to you for
> longer.
>
> Many thanks
> again — we were so glad you were c

Figure 64 Calm (around 130 l.p.m.)

Aerated writing
This pace — around 150 letters per minute — shows considerable attention to detail whilst the brain covers a great deal of ground, *so a versatile and capable mind* is suggested.

Rapid writing
Robert Saudek, the Czech graphologist who made a special study of speed, put rapid writing (more than 200 letters per minute) in the middle of his table! Beyond it came speeds we can describe as precipitated and carried away, and we have already seen samples of these (in Figs. 15 and 59).

Rapid writing shows an *enterprising spirit, a wish to embrace new events.* But what appears in good Form Level script as simplified or combined letter forms, can degenerate into a negligent, disorganized rush. Lively, intelligent adaptation becomes superficiality and a flight from introspection. Speed in good Form Level writing is frequently shown by the linking of i-dots, t-bars and other letters.

Rapid writing is recognized by these signs:

simplified, negligent or   increasing left margin
misplaced strokes

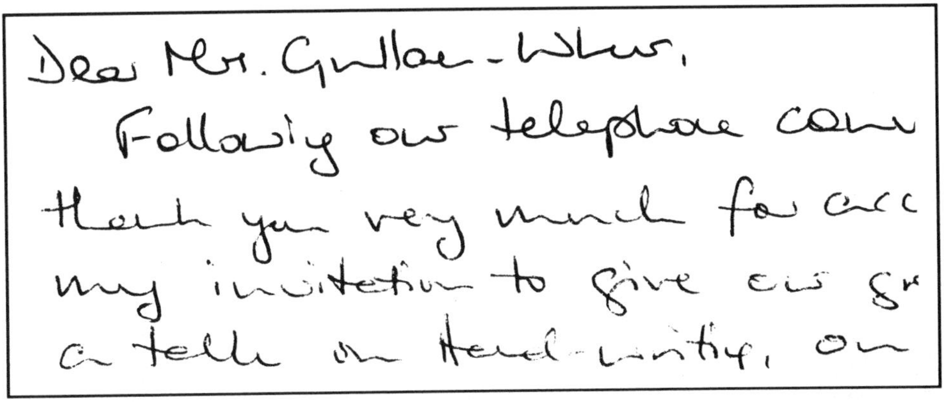

Dear Mr. Gullan-Whur,
Following our telephone conv
thank you very much for acc
my invitation to give our gr
a talk on hand-writing, on

Figure 65 Rapid (more than 200 l.p.m.)

the exclusion of leftward tendencies (below)

a noticeable disinclination to lift the pen

little variation in stroke direction

no initial strokes (page 105)

linked i-dots and t-bars

Let us remember that the speed of our writing can vary according to circumstances. The note we write before catching a bus will certainly show a lack of concern with surrounding factors — and a flight from introspection for that matter — but such qualities apply only to that one note. Make allowances for this.

Leftward Tendencies

We have seen that the progression across world space from left to right involves embracing the positive and the future, and that certain formations in the writing imply a reluctance to do this. The ancient symbolism of Yin and Yang in Fig. 28 shows that movements towards the left are more complex than simple retreat or inhibition: that discoveries of a kind less adventurous than those of the active world can be made in the passive, silent world of introspection, and that they add to our wisdom.

This does not mean that all leftward movements in the writing are reflective or self-aware. E. Singer comments, 'The man of common sense, the collector and the contemplative person as well as the greedy, the envious, the egotistical, will be amongst the left tendency writers.' But

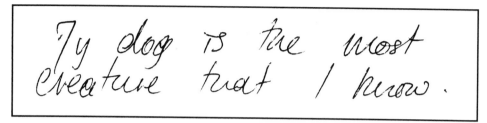

Figure 66   Ovals — leftward tendencies

because this aspect of writing generally provokes gloomy — if not damning — remarks, I want to impress the positive role of leftward tendencies at once.

A headmistress recently asserted, 'We train our girls to face forward.' Everyone knew what she meant: no unwholesome introspection or worrying solitary mooching. Yet, unacknowledged and unexplored, the unconscious mind can make itself felt in troublesome outbursts. Ania Teillard speaks of a natural turning towards the past and the profound in the second phase of life, when a position in society has been established and the libido begins to lose power. Strongly leftward tendencies in the writing of very young people hint at a recoil from the building phase of life, but such writers are actually best helped to look forward by help from those hidden areas to which they have turned. Let us acquire a little Eastern respect for them.

In strongly right-facing script, small intermittent leftward movements are probably unconscious. The holding-back shown in *ovals* of the a, o

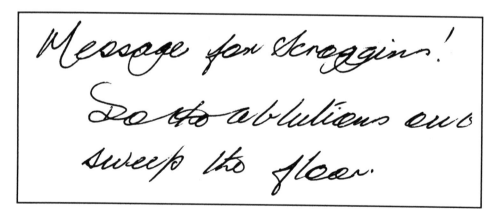

Figure 67   Leftward tendencies: ovals, lassos

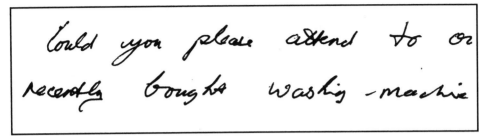

Figure 68 Leftward tendencies: lassos and downstrokes

and g in Fig. 66 indicate discretion, a hoarding of information about the self. The writing is dynamic and progressive but for this one sign.

The right slant of Figs. 66, 67 and 68 does not exclude characteristics associated with the left, and these samples show several. Fig. 67 shows spasmodic but strong leftward movements. Fig. 67 symbolizes effort and desire to progress into world space, but constant leftward tendencies make this difficult for the writer.

Ovals signify discretion in good Form Level writing, but distrust, secrecy or concealment in poor script.

Intense leftward movements of this type show a pulling back and into the self — a capacity to encapture and retain.

The **lasso** may reach back into the past, upwards into an area of reserve and self-control (see the table on page 54), or downwards into materialism and self-interest. There is always a degree of anxiety and double-checking — a looking backwards over the shoulder which makes it hard for such writers to plunge fearlessly into life. They come into their own when put in positions of care-taking and checking, however, and backward/downward lassos signify a deep respect for money and property.

An appreciation of the value (cost to give) of both material and emotional possessions may mean that such writers expect a return in kind for anything they 'part with'.

This very common tendency shows a defensive buffer against social intrusion — discrimination in allowing people 'in'.

Once frequently found, this formation is now a sign of social fastidiousness, showing deference to one's tribe or peer group, pride and reserve.

Left-directed downstrokes show appetite and desire, earthy sensuality and sometimes a lack of physical discipline; qualities obnoxious to nineteenth-century French clergy but excellent for avoiding stress and, in moderation, for the health. (Understrokes are discussed further from page 97.)

When the movement to the left is checked or frustrated as in Figs. 4, 68 and 119, restiveness and frustrated desire is shown.

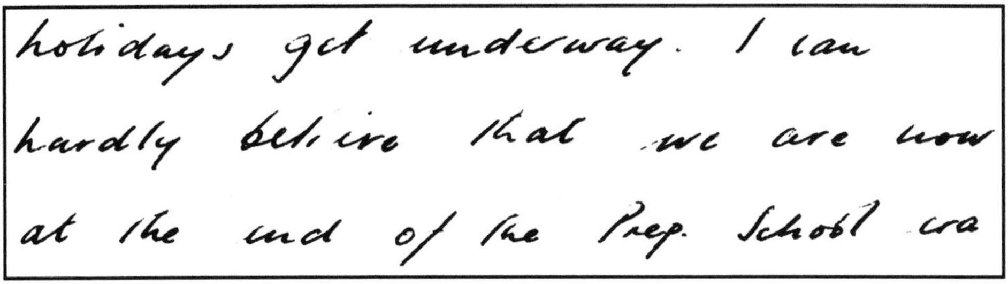

Figure 69 No left tendencies

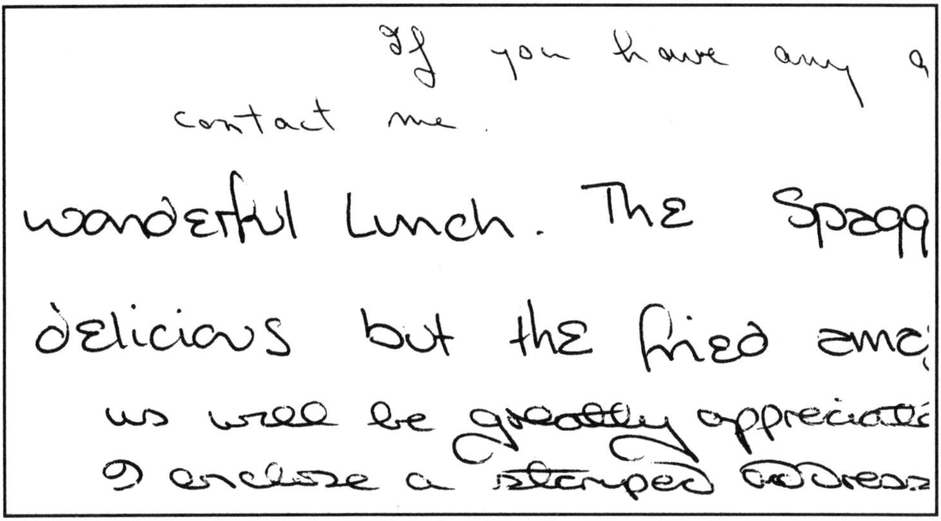

Figure 70 Left slant with leftward tendencies

Left slant and leftward tendencies together

This combination shows a fundamental refusal to accept the world and its values, though spontaneity and originality mark the writer who is prepared to impose his own tenacious standpoint quite fiercely. Such people may be prophets of alternative lifestyles, but poor Form Level writing suggests retreat, self-seeking or despair in the face of a world full of hostility, trickery and competition. Fig. 70 shows three separate examples.

Lack of leftward tendencies

This suggests a secure, trusting nature which questions neither itself nor the past, but advances into the world without inhibition. The manner of this optimistic progression depends entirely on the state of horizontal tension shown by the factors discussed from page 66 to this point, and by the general Form Level. Despite its lack of leftward movement, the writing of Fig. 69 shows considerable self-sufficiency and caution.

Resting Dots

As the writing moves across the page from left to right it impresses itself into the paper to a varying degree, leaving heavy or light strokes. The subject of *pressure* is bound up with stroke formation, and this precise study comes later in assessment, when we have formed a general picture of tendencies and are looking at smaller signs.

However, dots which appear in the body of the script but seem unrelated to it, being neither punctuation nor i-dots, are connected with horizontal tension. They mean that the writer is having difficulty in advancing; he is using a walking-stick which leaves a mark whenever he rests for a moment before interference with the brain's motor action, allows his pen to rest on the surface of the paper for an instant. However organized the writing may be, its writer is not finding the process of organization entirely easy.

Resting dots can be interpreted in relation to the script. In Fig. 9 they are caused by a combination of anxiety and neglect, but in Fig. 6 by stopping to correct letterforms and punctuation — again anxiety, but this time the movements are deliberate. True resting dots are formed unconsciously, and are generally thought to show some form of oppression or strained thinking.

Dots following signatures are not resting dots, but are usually unconsciously formed and are certainly necessary. *Anxiety and effort,* thoroughness and self-driving are indicated, and such dots are frequently found in a *thinking type* formation, as discussed on page 147.

Vertical Tension

The Three Zones

For at least 2,000 years man's nature has been considered by the wise to be a trinity of mind, body and spirit. Plato spoke at length of the need for these interacting forces to function in harmony, and of the dis-ease or non-health which results from their lack of balance.

We have seen that inhibition and unhappiness can prevent us from moving forward into world space, but we have not yet considered the

The Upper Zone	Idealism Aspiration Imagination
The Middle Zone	Sociability Self-esteem Expression of feeling Handling of the immediate Common sense
The Lower Zone	Practicality Sexuality Physical activity

powerful forces which, if acting against one another, can unbalance the whole.

Psychic energy tends to manifest itself in that area or zone of the writing in which it is most concentrated, and this may be as true of a single letter form as of a sheet of script. We may look at each of the three zones in turn and separately, but none can function in isolation: man's nature is threefold, and a concentration of psychic energy in one zone affects the other two. It may influence or decide the individual's life work, but he cannot live by it alone, and a zone which appears developed at the expense of the other two must indicate a lack of balance in the nature as a whole. (This principle is the basis of holistic medicine.)

The Middle Zone

Sociability

Self-esteem

Expression of the feelings

Handling of the immediate

Pragmatism — common sense

In this section we are dealing with rising and falling movements, assessing tendencies towards the upper, the spiritual, and the lower, the earth. We talk of uplifting thoughts and aspirations, and we know that down-to-earth, feet-on-the-ground attitudes represent the practical aspect of human behaviour. We shall see how pen movements become lower-based, lower directed and heavier in such impulses, and how they lighten, rise and climb when the mind occupies itself with higher matters, but we begin with that area of our lives which is central, immediate — set between past and future — and requires no climbing or descending.

D. H. Lawrence wrote of the 'single-storey mentality' of life on a bungalow estate, and whether or not he was justified in his remark, the analogy is a good one. The middle zone takes life head-on, and though we may neglect the upper and the lower zones of the mind, we are forced by the nature of our existence to 'live in' this area of ourselves. If we cannot, we must be put into the care of others, because this central level of life represents our own handling of the immediate, and without such consideration we become subhuman or superhuman.

The relatively large (tall) middle zone
When the middle zone is exaggerated in dimension, the writer tends to satisfy himself by his achievements in the rational, social, conscious and sentimental life. The **round** middle zone shows a significant interplay of feelings as we have seen, but the **angular** adherence to facts and a certain inflexibility. When the middle zone dominates, so do these qualities.

In high Form Level script an exaggerated middle zone may indicate competent handling of the here-and-now, and even in low Form Level writing it is a sign of social self-assurance. Returning to animal symbolism, an enlarged middle zone means a lion-proud nature, however well it may be masked.

Reduction of the upper and understrokes inevitably means low energy in those zones. The top sample in Fig. 71 shows some upper but no lower extension, and the other three some lower but no upper extension. Preoccupation with the immediate has led to neglect of the physical body and the higher reaches of the mind.

At times these areas are deliberately cut off or repressed, and this is shown by a hardening of the stroke ending; note the upper strokes of the second sample above.

The relatively small (short) middle zone
The reduced or undersized middle zone has a significance of its own, though we may be more impressed at first glance by the extended upper and lower strokes.

We have noted the social, sentimental or intellectual assurance indicated by an exaggerated middle zone, but here the aspirations (upper strokes) and physical demands (understrokes) are unmatched by everyday capability. Some graphologists attribute to this a profound

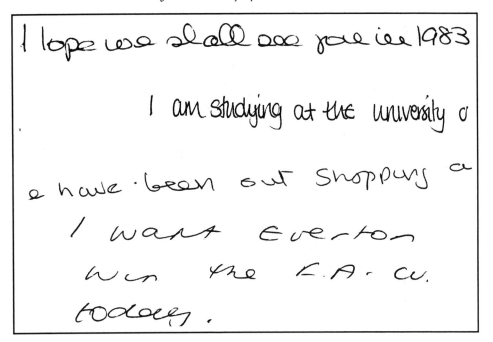

Figure 71 Exaggerated middle zone

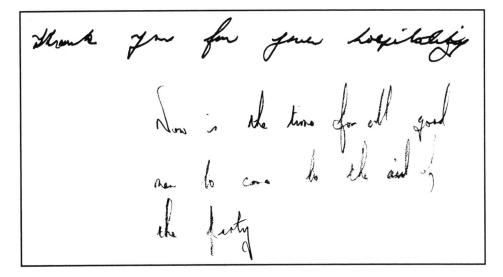

Figure 72 Undersized middle zone

sense of inferiority, often masked by a boastful or arrogant manner: there
is certainly a reduction in realism or head-on encounter. In high Form
Level script of this kind there may be a gift for translating a philosophy or
dream into earthy terms such as art, music of physical co-ordination, but
it will be at the expense of harmony in day-to-day living. In poor Form
Level writing we detect a Don Quixote mentality, where intensely
idealistic and physical demands may lead to unrealistic attitudes. (Note
the frustrated leftward turns and lassos in both the samples above.)

The Upper Zone

The upper strokes of the writing express that part of our nature which is
concerned with abstract dreams. For this reason, those who fix their gaze
on immediate objects and events, seldom lifting them to far horizons or
visions of the future, will tend to show restricted expression in that area.
The upper strokes will be meagre and soft, or, if higher thoughts are
glimpsed but consistently denied, they may be short and hard — as if
sawn off.

Idealism

Aspiration

Imagination

  The middle zone may display in itself an attitude towards the spiritual,
the upper. It may appear open to its influence (Figs. 17 and 54) or it may
pull away from the imagination, tending downwards to the earth, the
material (Figs. 37 and 116).
  We must remember that the upper zone may include attitudes not held
by angels. Bigoted moral stances, springing less from enlightenment than
from a desire to crush the desires of the world and the flesh below, may
produce in the writing hallmarks of the fanatic. Upper loops, dilated by
feeling, indicate principles and standards of a kind admired by Abbé
Michon and his followers, but which contain within their ethos a
damning and negative self-righteousness.
  When the giraffe looks down on us we cannot guess his thoughts. What
we do know is that he may be a little out of touch with events around his
waist or at his feet. He is unbalanced, yet with that lofty vision comes the

capacity for action beyond the reach of many. So it is with the upper zone in writing.

The exaggerated upper zone
When the upper zone is noticeably and habitually extended, the writer is preoccupied by ideas. He sees beyond the material and the social, and scorns mental precepts and feelings in favour of the abstract vision in his head. When this is closely tied to the realities of the lower zones and dominates them rather than totally rejecting them, the upper strokes will be well linked, but in poor Form Level writing and especially when the t-bars float adrift from the upright (Figs. 41 and 47) there may be at least temporary fanatical obsession.

Although French graphology consistently links the upper zone with spirituality, the principles of upward pen movement are chiefly tied to ideology and philosophy. Spirituality of a deeply searching nature is more often connected with leftward movement, and the extended upper zone more often seen in the writing of those who have 'found' than those who seek. It is often a sign of commitment to an ideal.

The undersized (short) upper zone
When the upper strokes end briefly or weakly above the middle zone, *little interest is shown in idealism or aspiration*: the writer finds fulfilment in

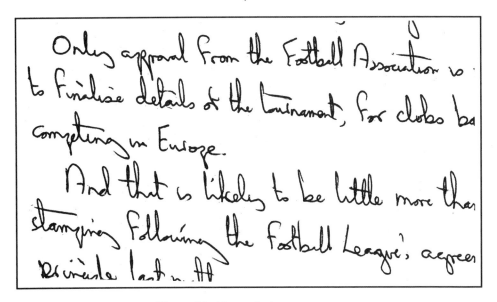

Figure 73 Extended upper zone

> *Reference our telephone converse*
> *for you to attend our meeting*
> *I would like to know exacly wl*
> *the price you charge.*
> *Please confirm in writing a*

Figure 74 Undersized upper zone

the material, sensual, social, emotional and intellectual areas of life. When the upper strokes are brief but hard, their abrupt endings show a deliberate abstention from upward movement, and this may indicate that whilst the writer contents himself with the immediate, it may not bring them fulfilment. He may be disillusioned by the philosophies he has tried out, and his earlier writing may show that at one time he was indeed preoccupied with higher thoughts. If he is young, he may be consciously or unconsciously rejecting a vocation.

The Lower Zone

When the pen plunges downwards towards the centre of the earth it concerns itself with the things of the earth, and these are all connected with survival, with the tangible areas reached by our five senses. They concern, if you like, our animal selves.

Practicality

Sexuality

Physical activity

Remembering the inseparable nature of the three parts of our human wholeness, we must not fall into the trap of supposing that high is good and low is bad; that if our writing shows strong expression of energy in the lower zone, we are somehow less evolved people. We may be artists, athletes or natural farmers.

The functions of the animal and material self are vital to our well-being, but like the other two parts or zones, must be maintained in balance if the nature of the whole is not to suffer. The animal which rootles, its nose never leaving the ground, may score high in the finding and hoarding of food but is missing a great deal. Similarly, the bird which never visits the earth for material sustenance cannot survive. As people we are structurally designed to live in all three zones, and we need what each has to offer.

Sudden changes in the formation of the lower zone may show alterations in health, and distortions of the lower strokes are associated with physical frustration and sexual difficulties. Links with actual physical trauma to the lower limbs are controversial, but many graphologists insist that specific illness is indicated in the three zones.

The extended (large) lower zone

A lower zone which, looped or not, appears disproportionately larger than the other zones, indicates *orientation to life through material, tangible objects and the five senses*. This necessarily implies a sober, materialistic, unimaginative and earthbound attitude, and the writer may feel threatened and insecure when these values are questioned. He is unlikely, for instance, to tolerate the mystical or airy-fairy products of abstract thought.

Leftward turned downstrokes, especially when very large, show a capacity for sensual enjoyment and physical 'taking'. The more they are controlled, looped back (Fig. 21) or shortened, the greater the degree of physical self-control. Right-turned downstrokes show energy put to productive, outgoing use. Figure-of-eight downstrokes (see Fig. 65) show immense practical resilience, and it is difficult to reconcile this interpretation of them with the concept of aesthetic appreciation promoted by some graphologists, though there may be a link.

Sexual tendencies as shown in handwriting are a study in themselves; see Patricia Marne's *Crime and Sex in Handwriting*. The enlargement of the lower zone indicates only that considerable psychic energy is directed to bodily appetites or expression.

The undersized (short) lower zone

When the downstrokes are small in comparison with the other zones, *little energy is being expressed physically*. If the downstrokes are weak and taper away at the ends (Fig. 120) the writer has no interest in the earthier aspects of living, but when the endings are hard (clubbed) as below, expression of energy is blocked and there is a risk of injury to health. Viewing the stroke as an electrical impulse from the brain, it is easy to see

I haven't a clue what I'll
be doing tonight but I
won't be spending much
money whatever it is

Figure 75   Extended lower zone

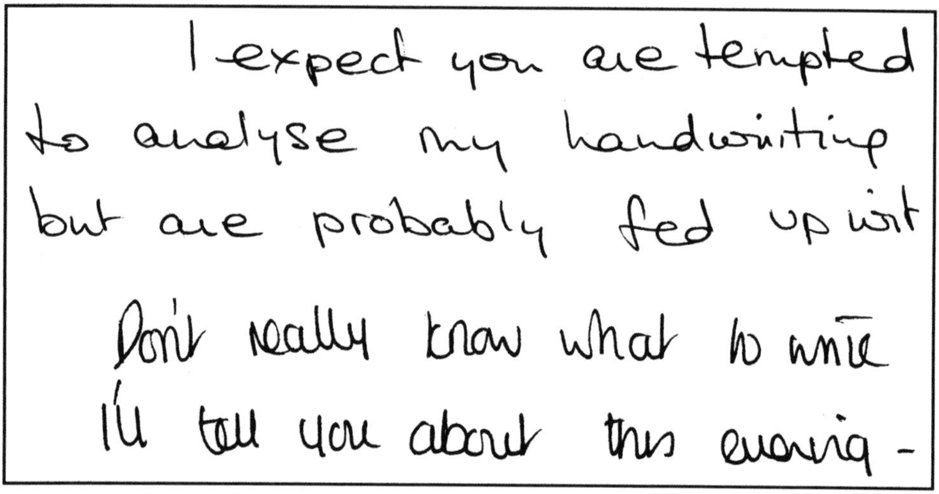

I expect you are tempted
to analyse my handwriting
but are probably fed up wit
Don't really know what to write
I'll tell you about this evening –

Figure 76   Undersized lower zone

how abruptly the pen is being withdrawn from the lower zone, and that distaste for that area of living is based in the mind rather than the body.

An undersized lower zone suggests that the writer denies himself the comfort or distraction of purely physical or material activity. He is unable to escape from himself as a mental and social being into abandoned sensual or manual delights — for the use of tools is included in physical expression — so cannot forget himself. It is remarkable that the writing of the physically disabled, while showing inhibition of motor activity and therefore of organization, gives frequent evidence of joyful and satisfying physical expression. Often, a greater awareness of the body leads to appreciation and increased use of it.

Graphology paints a picture of the concentration of our energies.

Entanglement

Irregularity of zone dimension may involve a subtle interpretation of the expression of psychic energy, and this is discussed on page 85 in the section on **regularity**.

When the upper strokes and downstrokes of consecutive lines become mingled and encroach on one another's space, the script is said to be **entangled**.

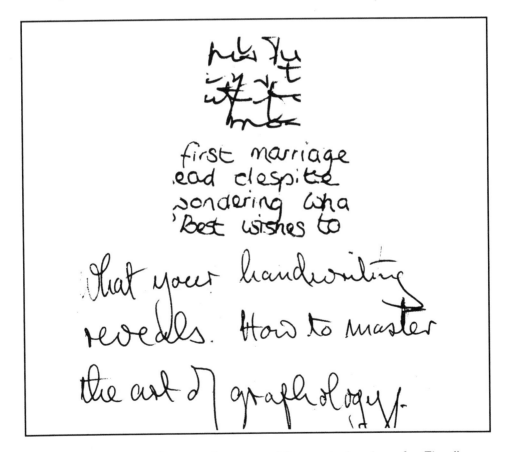

Figure 77 Entanglement of upper and lower strokes (see also Fig. 4)

Teillard believes this tendency to mean that the emotions rule over reason, that the writer is agitated and (at least temporarily) blinded by his feelings. Since the upper strokes are always superimposed on the downstrokes (physical expression), I find entanglement to indicate an attempt at imposing discipline on the powerful lower impulses which the writer feels may engulf him. From this point of view, entanglement is a form of **retouching** (see page 116).

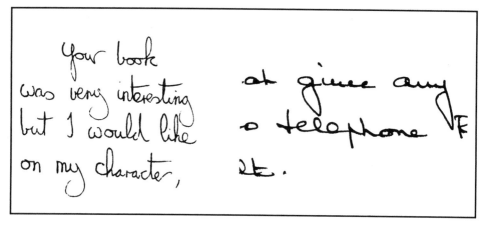

Figure 78   Entanglement avoided

Space symbolism suggests that the writer dislikes leaving his own tracks, and feels safer in maintaining contact with his own earlier movements. It also implies that 'down the page' is not safe, and this ties in with a fear of engulfing lower impulses.

Saudek found entanglement of upper and lower zones in the writing of great men — Kant and Beethoven — and it is also evident in letters written by Galilei, Elizabeth I and Brahms. (See *What Your Handwriting Reveals*.) Can it be, then, that those whose vision shows them irresistible goals almost beyond their reach, sometimes screw their hearts and courage to the sticking-point in order to reach them? Do they, perhaps, create in themselves *a degree of obsession* composed of inspiration, will and emotion? Entanglement is generally found in dynamic writing: the lower zone contributes ample psychic energy but inspiration and imagination cut across it, denying its potential domination of the mind.

Many — most — writers do not deny the lower zone its full share of expression, and may carefully avoid interference in its role, as shown in Fig. 78.

Entanglement has not as yet been clearly interpreted, but the speculations above include French, German and American ideas besides my own.

Baselines
Lines of print in books are perfectly straight, but lines of writing produced by human hand are subject to outside interference and mental turbulence. Those who write in consistently straight lines tend to be of even if not phlegmatic temperament (see Figs. 55 and 64), but most of us are capable of producing them at times.

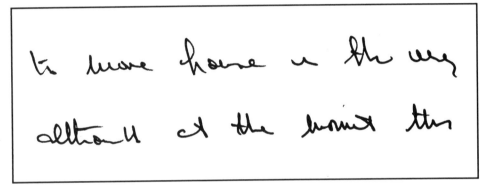

Figure 79 Rising baseline

The baseline (line slope) of the script is a barometer of mood, and is perhaps more prone to sudden change than any other facet of the writing. It can vary from day to day, sample to sample, and even within a couple of lines, since it indicates a rising or falling of the spirits according to current thoughts and feelings.

Script which rises as it progresses to the right shows *a lifting of the spirits*, optimism and hope. The table on page 54 also suggests self-confidence and ambition, but a habitually rising signature is a far more reliable indication of this. An upward baseline trend requires energy, so is a sign of current buoyancy.

The baseline descends to the right *when debility or demoralization causes the spirits to sink*, and this may happen for weeks on end — or for certain words only if they cover a depressing topic. The script is moving towards that part of the table (page 54) concerned with negativity and pessismism, and all movements in the writing which take this downward/forward plunge resemble the shuffling, head-bowed gait of the hopeless. But

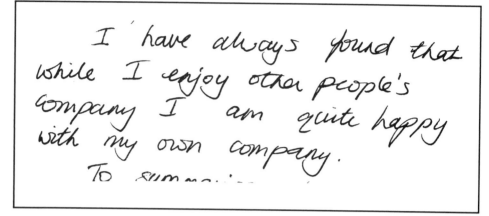

Figure 80   Falling baseline

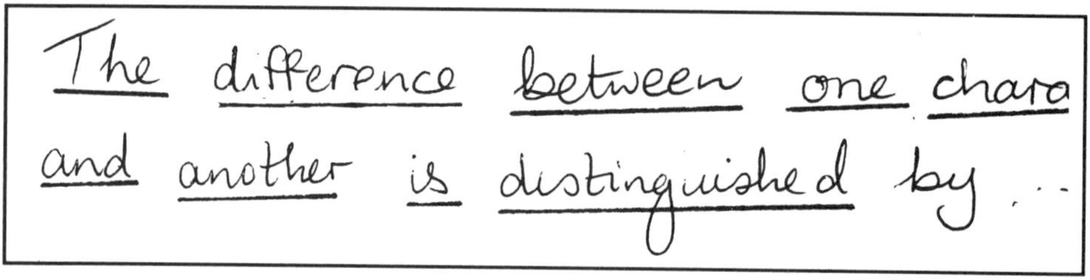

The difference between one chara
and another is distinguished by ...

Figure 81   Tiled baseline

tiredness alone can be responsible for a falling baseline, and we should remind ourselves of this before taking apparent despondency too seriously.

Minor fluctuations in the baseline are of interest. **A wavy baseline** shows mental turbulence and effort, and is often caused by emotional involvement in the subject matter. If wavy baselines are habitual the writer may be moody or unstable, but many samples must be checked before deciding this. There may be other *irregular* features in the writing (see page 142). **Tiled baselines** indicate bursts of effort and short-lived optimism, again probably due to temporary conditions. Attempts at lifting the writing or the spirits fail constantly, yet are repeatedly initiated.

Lined paper controls the vertical tension of the baseline, making this aspect of graphology impossible to interpret.

Small Signs

Beauchataud calls these free features, since they are not directly concerned with the creation of alphabetical forms. When the writer is attempting to produce legible writing, he must do so by arranging the letters of the alphabet into recognizable patterns — just as this sentence appears in print. But he makes certain other pen movements which are omitted from print, or which are not bound by rules of legibility, and these, like spacing, slant, margins and speed, allow inner attitudes to be freely expressed.

Most of these small *free* signs are bound up in space symbolism since their movements relate to the treatment of world space. They tend to be habitual, and although several variations may be seen in one sample, they form a recognizable pattern within themselves.

The mental approach to the subject in hand must be taken into account in case it has deeply influenced the writer. This is true of all assessment, and it is also true that some of us are very much more affected by changing conditions or new circumstances than others. Writing being to some extent a barometer of mood, the 'free' signs may reflect this. The vertical tension of t-bars, for instance, may be subject to exactly the same rules of impulse as the baseline.

Other small signs may embody such unique formations that they are truly identification marks, and it is in this respect that the most calligraphic or copybook of styles yields up its individuality to a careful graphologist.

Word beginnings

The way we begin each word or collection of letter forms shows *our approach to new encounters*. It may be consistent in its alacrity or its timidity, or subject to stop-start changes of mood, but a pattern of behaviour is always present.

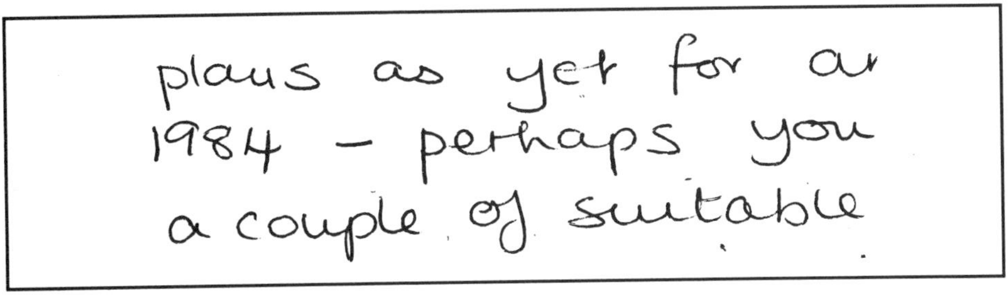

Figure 82 No initial strokes

No initial (cautionary) strokes. Writing which habitually launches into each word with no extra pen movements or embellishments of the first letter shows *a direct and resourceful approach*. The writer makes quick decisions, goes straight to the point, and is not perturbed by sudden new demands. I have found this sign linked to successful spontaneity in public life, in broadcasting and any active media work (Fig. 82).

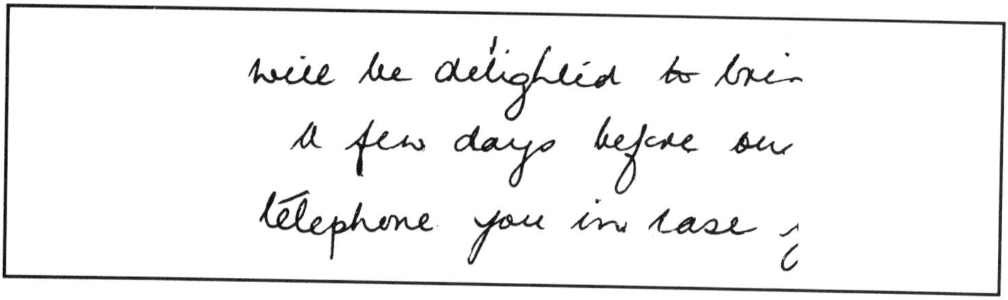

Figure 83   Initial strokes and hooks

Initial strokes and hooks. Hooks at the beginning of words show that the writer *is hanging on to something* (Fig. 83). He may be unwilling to 'let go' or launch himself, and this is accentuated by the presence of resting dots.

Low-based initial strokes. This type of caution originates in the hoarding and retaining area, and if the hooks are strong it shows acquisitiveness. It may also show systematic objection to new ideas.

High hooks. *Pride* is the reason for caution here. There may be a fastidious reluctance to mingle or partake in common activity — a fear of losing face or departing from past dignity.

Word endings

These show our *attitude towards ending one action and beginning another*, and are often tied to social behaviour. There is more agreement about the meaning of downward plunging end-strokes than over upturned strokes and hooks, but it is generally agreed that hooks at both the beginnings *and* ends of words indicate a character who is hard to persuade or dissuade!

Abrupt endings. Word endings which habitually form a curt downward movement express a negative attitude (see page 29), but its precise nature is usually most clearly decided by other signs or patterns in the writing. Very short strokes (see Fig. 23) may indicate reticence or discretion rather than withholding, but **deeply plunging endings** involve the physical senses and mean a deliberate digging in of the toes or a desire to realize something concrete.

Downward curves (sometimes described as an *s* formation) make continual *reference to self-interest* (see page 29) of a physical or materialistic kind. Beauchataud sees this movement as 'monopolizing'.

Upward curves show a lifting of the spirits in some form of inspiration, but this must be taken in conjunction with other signs and patterns, since motives may range from cheerful optimism through religion to proud calculation (see page 54).

Horizontally stretched endings are the subject of controversy. Interpretations range from love of gossip (Teillard) to a desire to prolong the present moment. The general principle — often so vital in making a portrait or analysis — is one of *enjoyment of the immediate*.

The formation of beginnings and endings of words may be closely related to the subject matter of the text. Look at several samples if possible.

t-bars

The crossing of the letter t plays an important role in British and American graphology, and was comprehensively covered in *What Your Handwriting Reveals*. For Beauchataud its significance is tied to other similar movements in the writing since it proceeds from the same impulses, but her definitions of its variations are concerned, like the British, with purposefulness, will and drive. This force or resolution (of the lack of it) is connected with the future itself, rather than with other people: remembering the animal symbolism of earlier on, we are talking about the way we set our eyes or our sights on the horizons before us. Before assessing a t-bar it is important to know whether the writer is left- or right-handed.

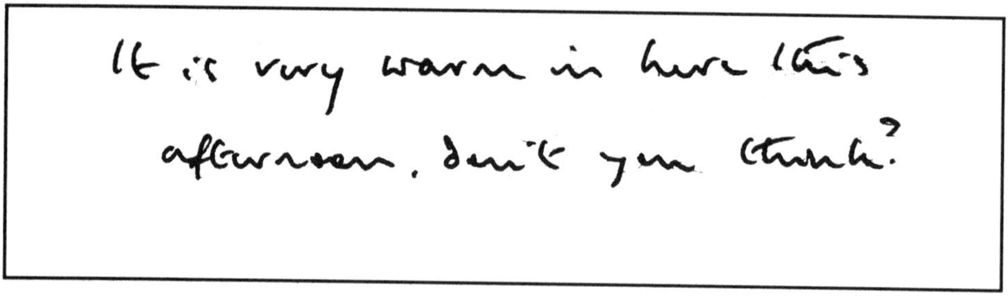

Figure 84   T-bar to the right of the upright

Rather than depicting the many differing forms a t-bar can take, let us consider a few general principles. Does the t-bar show a forward and direct vision, or is it twisted backwards, downwards or upwards? Is the bar present at all? If not, see page 113. Is it continually linked to things nearer and more immediate than the far horizon, or is it floating freely without any links at all, even to its own upright stroke? The t-bar is more than another type of word ending: besides being a *statement of vision or intention* it can be described as *a barometer of vitality and will*.

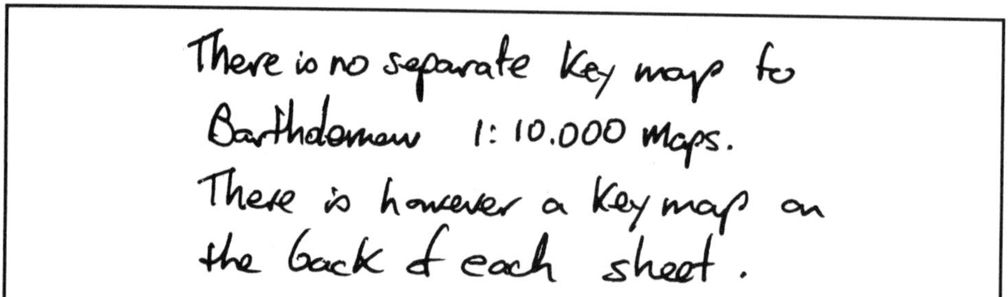

Figure 85   T-bar precisely crossing the upright

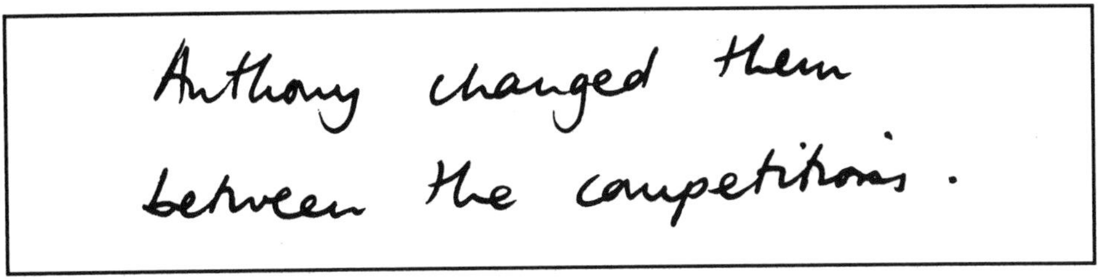

Figure 86 Consistently linked t-bar

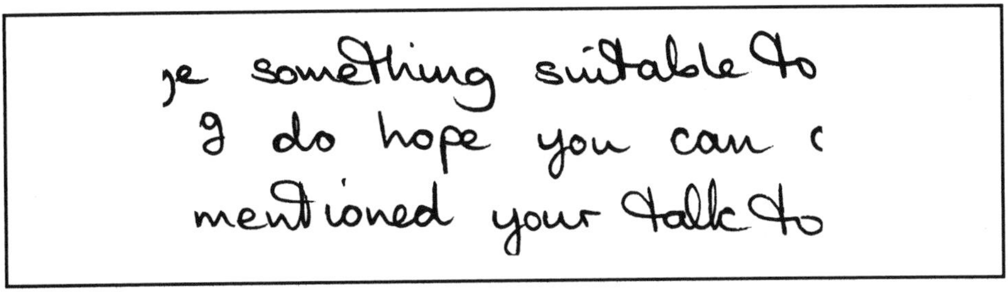

Figure 87 T-bars forming lassos

It also indicates our relationship with fact. T-bars like those in Figs. 14 and 84 show drive which is *out of touch* with reality. If **the bars float to the right**, plans are eager but are not being implemented — a sign often but not always related to the writing of the elderly. When the bars are **above the upright** (see Fig. 41) the vision is too lofty for realistic planning: this pie-in-the-sky sign can be the mark of a fanatic, or of someone with a mission for which they are less well-equipped than they suppose.

t-bars to the left of the upright show slow response and a tendency to procrastinate. Conversely if the t-bar is as **precise as printface**, no matter how disorganized the writing or weird the subject, the writer's mind is meticulously applied and exercising scientific precision (Figs. 11 and 85). The extent of his forcefulness depends partly on the length of the bar and partly on its *pressure* — an aspect of graphology still to be discussed.

A forceful t-bar may penetrate the future like an arrow, or it may **link itself to a following letter** as in Fig. 86. Such writers tend to have minds which move forward in logical stages rather than far-sighted bounds: they can adapt quickly to new information but may bend it to suit their mental concepts, which are often powerfully accurate and ambitious. This is especially true when t-bars link words.

Sometimes the t-bar is **linked from the base**. This controversial sign should be interpreted discretely: its general principle is one of common sense, practical logic or earthy purposefulness, and graphologists who call this deceit or cunning must be very sure that other signs in the writing confirm it.

Firmness in t-bars is connected with health as well as spiritual zest, and bars which point in the direction of negativity (⟶) show weariness rather than obstinacy if they are fragile.

Bent or bowed t-bars show inconstancy of drive: the will does not shoot forwards like an arrow but, like a boomerang, may rebound from the direction in which it is aimed. Again, much depends on pressure and length. When the bar is forced backwards before moving on to the right, the general principle involved is entrenchment or reference to the past. Pride or anxiety may figure in interpretation (Fig. 87), but the habitual creator of such lassos or triangles may be relied on for his thoroughness. His will is directed towards that which lies in his grasp.

t-bars formed from right to left may be a sign of left-handedness. The direction of the stroke affects interpretation, so ask if possible.

The higher placed the t-bar, the stronger is the inspiration of the individual spirit. Low-based t-bars seek safety in the tried and tested, and so may show a lack of self-confidence (Fig. 65).

A diversity of t-bar formations shows versatility of drive and subtlety of approach in high Form Level script, but in feeble or low Form Level writing one mode of approach may cancel out the effectiveness of the other (Fig. 16).

Because t-bars can be a barometer showing the *current application of energy*, either check several samples or modify any comment on them by making this clear.

Capitals

Capital letters are used less in the English language than in many others, and are considered significant. Their formation is generally quite different from lower-case letters, and each individual's treatment of them reflects his approach to accepted norms of Importance and Authority. (These capitals deliberately emphasize a natural tendency to insert one as a mark of respect: see Fig. 45!)

As symbols of space usage, capital formations show unconscious attitudes connected with our willingness — or otherwise — to defer to authority. They also show in what areas our sense of importance does actually lie. These are not strictly speaking social attitudes, though they will of course affect our behaviour, but a *matching of our own importance against generally accepted claims to importance*. French psychologists see this as a graphological portrait of the *ego* state.

Other graphologists rightly suggest that capital letters need no analysis if they are neither over-large nor undersized, nor inharmonious — containing exaggerated movements. Unfortunately they do not always agree on the meaning of dimension differences. Generally speaking, **over-large capitals** *demand and defer to authority*: they see it as a good thing and they envy those who wield it. They often accompany an undersized middle zone (Figs. 4, 72 and 73), and their pretentious size may mask feelings of inferiority. But in generally large, good Form Level writing, they are an aspect of confident self-projection. It is easy to see from these examples that dimension must take into account many other factors in the writing.

In general, **small capitals** suggest a writer who *neither needs nor accepts authority*. He may be extraordinarily arrogant or of saintly humility: other signs and patterns in the writing will decide which (see Figs. 7 and 46). To return briefly to our animal image, we need only note to what extent each individual *alters his attitude* in response to the demands of authority (his own included) as he crosses world space.

The following variations are generally noted by graphologists. All unusual formations can be analysed in terms of space symbolism as in *What Your Handwriting Reveals*, but these small signs are regularly found.

Capitals which **plunge downwards as they end** are similar to other plunging endings. See page 107.

The peaked cap or protecting arm which stretches out over following letters represents a patriarchal or matriarchal attitude, combining *authority with protection*.

Capitals which **attempt to underline** the following letters are thought by French graphologists to signify vanity (see Fig. 2).

When the capital is **combined with the next letter** various interpretations may be made. Often this happens in writing which is inventively linked throughout — the *combiné* script so highly regarded by the French. True, the rightward tendencies involved in the linking of capitals may suggest altruism, and the need for spontaneity and speed imply intelligence, but since all rightward movements indicate only a general principle of *looking outwards and forwards*, we must examine all other signs and patterns before imputing moral value to this sign. (See Figs. 3, 5, 50 and 119).

Simple, **typographic capitals** suggest aesthetic intelligence but may contain some of the quality of calligraphic writing.

Capitals in the middle of words imply suspect judgement of Importance!

i-dots

i-dots are an aspect of punctuation, but they have a particular significance. They indicate the writer's *capacity for concentration and accuracy*, and as such can be an important part of analyses connected with professional ability. Idiosyncrasies in i-dotting — fully covered in *What Your Handwriting Reveals* — are of secondary importance to their presence and their positioning in relation to the stalk of the letter.

The omission of i-dots is due to negligent attention to detail. In rapid writing it shows haste and impatience, and in slow script a lack of organization: if it is habitual the writer will probably commit 'sins of omission' in all aspects of his life, since he is not basically painstaking or watchful of detail. But see page 113.

Close i-dots show a *capacity for accurate detail*, especially if they are invariably close to the stalk. The anxiety said by some graphologists to be an aspect of such precision is perhaps better described as fussiness. The full stop after a signature discussed on page 53 is an extension of this trait.

Speed and pressure will alter the shape of the dot, and it may become linked to the next letter — or to a preceding t-bar, as in Fig. 55. The **linked i-dot** may be a sign of intelligent or logical combination of ideas but this graphologist still finds it consistent with a sardonic or satirical sense of the ridiculous. (In space symbolism it represents a dragging away from the ideal (upper) to the logical and concrete zones.)

Movement in the i-dot is traditionally associated with a fertile or idealistic imagination, especially if the dots are in a high position, but speed and dragging of the pen must be taken into account: the movement may be a rightward one rather than an upward arc. Continental graphologists have additional marks — accents — over certain letters to take into consideration, and whilst it is possible to define the meaning of each arc or extended i-dot, they must on the whole be taken as part of a general movement in the writing. We can safely add to this the principle that habitually hard, square or rigid i-dots indicate a rigid outlook — from a reverence for attested facts to blindly positive assertiveness on all

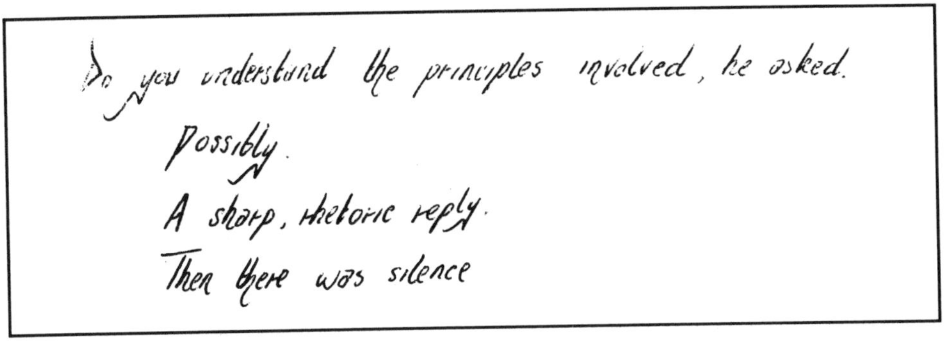

Figure 88 Omission of i-dots

matters. **Soft or fluid i-dots**, wherever they may be placed, show flexibility and tolerance, but sometimes less strength of character or resolve. The i-dot forms part of the overall jigsaw, and must be considered in relation to other patterns.

Usually, the shape or movement of i-dots, as well as their positioning, is unconscious. Occasionally they provide a wanted opportunity for self-expression, as in Fig. 51 which usually attracts the attention it desires.

This is a *deliberate form of self-projection or egotism*, and should be considered as an embellishment. See page 136.

Other i-dot forms are an aspect of stroke quality, which is discussed in Section III. Small single movements have a significance of their own, as is shown by the wide variation of t-bars in writing, and we shall come to this.

As in most aspects of analysis, one sample of writing is not sufficient to make an overall judgement of character. Much depends on circumstances — on the directing of the mind at the time of writing. Fig. 86, for instance, shows uncharacteristic i-dots and baseline: the writer is in an inspired and eager state. Fig. 59 is from the same writer on another occasion. See also pages 140–4.

Punctuation

The dotting of the i serves as a good example of attitude to accuracy, but it also gives an idea of the *degree of attention* paid by the writer to true and correct presentation. Whatever the positioning, shape or texture of the i-dots, it is easy to tell at a glance whether they are placed with care, or whether they are neglected.

In studying punctuation as a whole we embrace many aspects of graphology. We return to the question of organization and Form Level, and we anticipate the lessons of Section III on regularity, letter and stroke formation and pressure. Nevertheless, the small additional marks of punctuation are correctly placed under **Small Signs**, particularly in the French category of free features.

Small they may be, but the psychological importance of punctuation marks is great. Besides being a barometer of a current state of mind — punctuation can go to the winds in the most caring of hands when external excitement distracts the mind from details — it also reflects deep and permanent attitudes towards accepted fact and communication. We shall be returning to the matter of attention and neglect in Section III, but in this broader concept we are looking at more than form. **The omission of almost all punctuation** (if it is not exceptional and caused by a particular spontaneous impetus such as euphoria or extreme haste) may indicate several quite different states of mind, so be very careful before making any judgement at all. It is not true to say that it indicates a lack of interest in accuracy: pressure of time may force a writer to commit something of immense factual importance to paper with no precision at all. (If you suspect you have been given something of this nature to analyse ask about the circumstances. Fig. 17 shows a high degree of intelligent caring, but several i-dots and t-bars are missing.) Look at other samples before deciding that negligent punctuation is habitual.

Even if it is, snap judgements are still out of the question. There are aspects which the most experienced of graphologists will have to puzzle over. For instance, is the negligence deliberate, as may be the case in Fig. 88? Perhaps — as in the books of James Joyce and other modern novelists or poets — there is a positive intention to transcend such small and petty matters in the pursuit of an inspired train of thought. (See also Fig. 55.)

We must not confuse a distaste for details with a lack of awareness of them. When the words are clear and legible whilst punctuation is sparse we can *suspect* some kind of conscious aversion, and it is reasonable to ask the writer about it. The reply is often, 'My punctuation's never been good', implying that they know and do not care. This, then is deliberate.

Sometimes clarity and communication are not desired at all, and this will be discussed under **Legibility**. Evasiveness or deliberate obscurity is a possibility, but a charge we should not make lightly. See also illegible **Signatures**.

As pointed out at the beginning of this passage, lack of punctuation does not mean absence of anxiety, but **excessive punctuation** does usually mean that *some kind of intensity is present*. Meticulous punctuation shows a high degree of attention and desire for accuracy, but it may equally show a wish to be seen to do things correctly. This may result in a pedantic accentuation of each mark — large commas, slightly excessive use of speech-marks and exclamation marks, and so on. There will

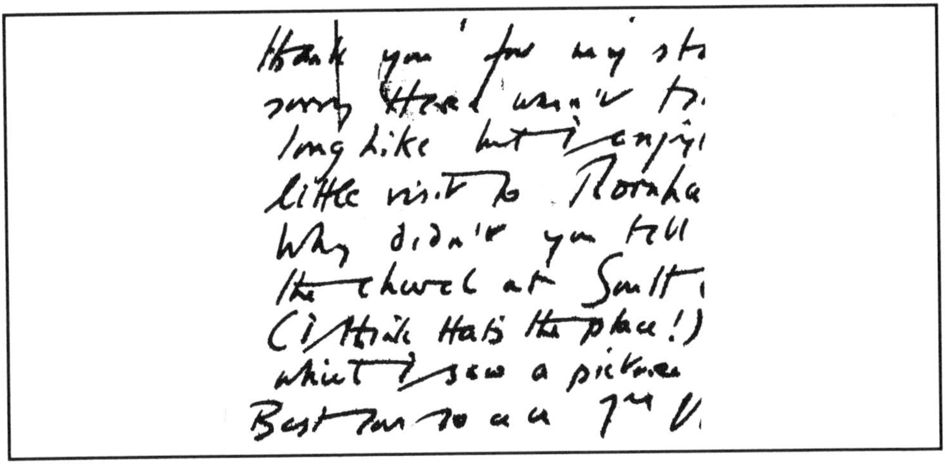

Figure 89 Excessive punctuation in good form level writing

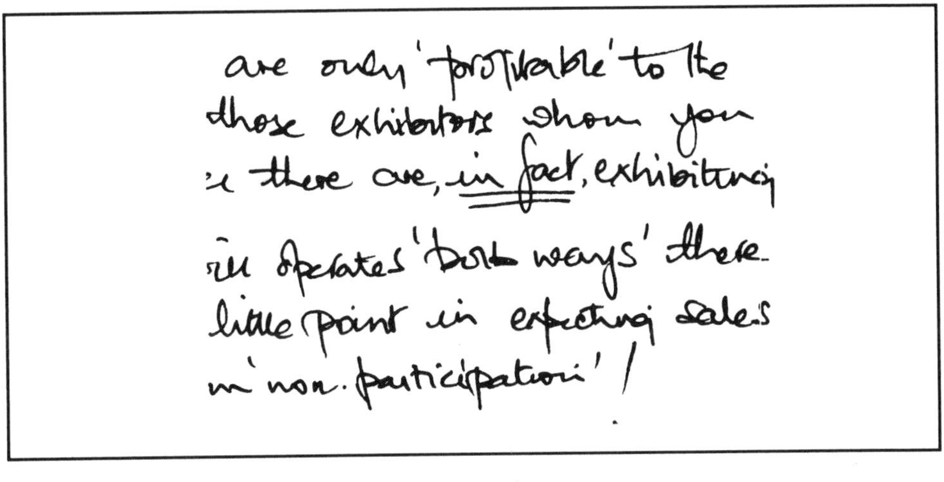

Figure 90 Excessive punctuation

usually be other signs of image-making (projection of the persona as opposed to the genuine self) in the writing. If this slightly exaggerated punctuation is accompanied by wide margins all round, calligraphic writing and enlarged capitals, the writer probably sets great store on appearances, and goes to great length to avoid losing face. The signature of this individual will back up such a portrait or modify it. (See Fig. 89.) (Singer suggests that over-punctuation implies snobbery.)

Excessive punctuation in low Form Level writing betrays an anxiety to be correct or to be approved. The writer is trying to communicate clearly, and may even write entirely in capitals. In high or low level script, excessive punctuation can signify a love of drama or a bid for attention (see Fig. 90).

Retouching

Anxiety is certainly present when the writer continually returns to make small corrections or additions to words (see Fig. 91). The reason behind this action may be an exaggerated desire to get things right, but there are times when such retouching seems out of character, and graphologists may in some circumstances see this as a guilty conscience — the mark of someone who has something to hide. Generally, however, it is accompanied by such signs as an unnecessary full stop after the signature, showing a fussy, anxious nature. Retouching may feature amid a host of admirable characteristics, as in Fig. 91, and suggests Adler's theory of constant disapproval in early childhood leading to low self-esteem. In aggressive or calligraphic writing, the trait is more suspicious, but do not start imputing criminal tendencies until you have practised graphology for many years!

Covering strokes

These occur when the writer repeats a particular stroke or pen movement

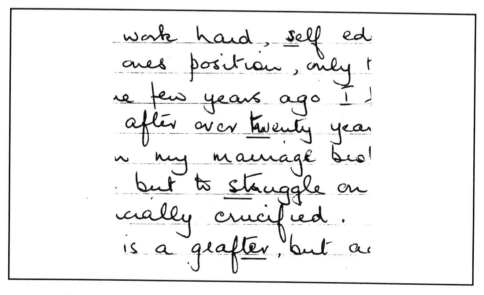

Figure 91 Retouching. Four examples have been underlined

before continuing with the script, sometimes producing circles within circles or double lines. (See Fig. 67.) The movement inhibits speed and spontaneity, and represents prudence or discretion, an unwillingness to 'open up' to others. Its leftward direction and lack of forward movement may suggest wariness or — in conjunction with other signs — stealth.

Signatures: the Self-Image

Whilst the writing of one's own name is subject to all the principles of analysis covered so far, it retains a unique character and importance in graphology. In its capacity as a directly visual representation of the self-image, H. J. Jacoby saw it as a psychological visiting-card. It reflects *the attitude which the individual adopts in the face of society* (Beauchataud), rather than the true self whose nature is manifested in the general script, and so must always be considered in relation to the rest of the writing.

As symbols of space usage, signatures were discussed comprehensively in *What Your Handwriting Reveals*. In this workbook we are looking for a general principle through which the extraordinary differences and embellishments in signatures can be interpreted, and I believe Beauchataud's definition above to be the most useful. And though Continental graphology frowns upon the analysing of signatures in isolation, that is, in autograph form or as an addition to typewritten letters, to a large extent this principle can justly be applied to these symbols of self-image — just so long as it is constantly borne in mind that they reflect not the character, but the pose.

Because signatures represent the attitude adopted by the individual, an instant and dramatic revelation is made by putting the word 'me' in place of the name. A few genuine signatures have been included in this chapter, but on the whole the use of 'me' or 'me and my family/status', can better illustrate the way signatures are presented. The forename alone, written on relatively intimate documents, is 'me': the forename and surname together represent 'me' in the family unit. Affection, dependence or abhorrence towards this extended self can be markedly clear in a full signature.

The formation of each part of the signature grows in maturity to the extent to which it matters publicly, and this growth may be uneven. Those who continue their education in an advanced or prolonged way are less likely to consider the importance of their signature than those who use it to validate business transactions soon after leaving school at sixteen. Much repetition makes the signature automatic, and sadly the glamorous self-image so carefully contrived during early adolescence can become an established but ridiculous signature, reflecting nothing but

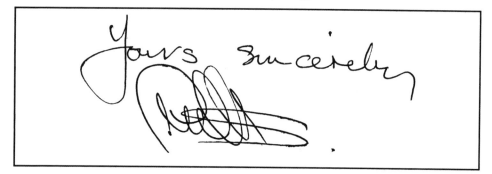

Figure 92 Inharmonious with text

immature yearnings. Substituting 'me' for the signature soon shows it up for what it is.

Signature inharmonious with the text
Although Fig. 92 has other significant features which we shall come to in due course, we stay for the moment with the all-important relationship of the signature to the rest of the script. Fig. 92 shows a signature which is a *false self-image*. Far from being a simple statement of fact, as in Fig. 93, it is a scream of outrage and anguish and only to be truly understood in terms of character revealed in the many lines which precede it. Fig. 93, in contrast shows sufficient self-confidence for the writer to avoid embellishing, exaggerating or projecting any particular image: an identification is required and therefore supplied — and this is the chief purpose of a signature.

Figure 93 Harmonious with text

Signature in harmony with the text

In Fig. 93 we find complete *harmony between what the person thinks she is like and what she really is like*. Such harmony is found in both high and low Form Level script (proving that we need not fear to describe the most copybook of styles as harmonious if it answers the simple criterion of freedom from exaggeration, contraflow and embellishment). This type of signature represents a good degree of self-knowledge: there is no gulf between the interior and the exterior experience of life, and therefore — though other signs and patterns in the writing may modify this — no severe mental conflict.

Beauchataud 'judges' a signature by its firmness, harmony and simplicity. I hope that we do not judge at all, but note with compassion the difficulty experienced by some people in relating to the world from an effortlessly natural standpoint. We have talked much of space symbolism and the way in which we approach and cross world space: signatures concern our bearing towards those we encounter along the way. If we are afraid of them or try hard to impress them, it will be for a reason — outdated and irrelevant though that reason may be.

Signature dimension in relation to the text

A signature can only be large or small in relation to the normal writing of that individual. A large **signature — larger than any other word** on the written page — shows *Self-importance*: the writer counts himself the most noteworthy presence around. The same applies if the signature is tall rather than dilated, but we have learned that where the middle zone is small, as in Fig. 94, confidence is only skin deep and this may result in bluster or boasting.

A very **small signature in relation to the rest of the script** may show

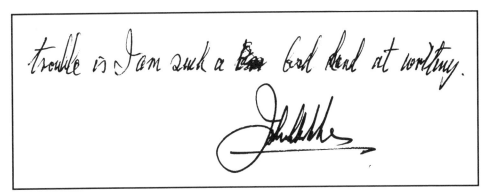

Figure 94 Pseudo-large signature

modesty or timidity. In high Form Level writing the writer may be fully satisfied with his own inner mental resources and desire chiefly *not* to be noticed. He may be far from timid, as other signs and patterns will show. But when the signature is not only small but also placed left of centre on the page, a modest attitude to that particular subject at any rate is implied.

A **spaced-out signature** (see page 66) shows *a forward-reaching, world-embracing attitude* with nothing to hide or fear. Fig. 95 shows confidence

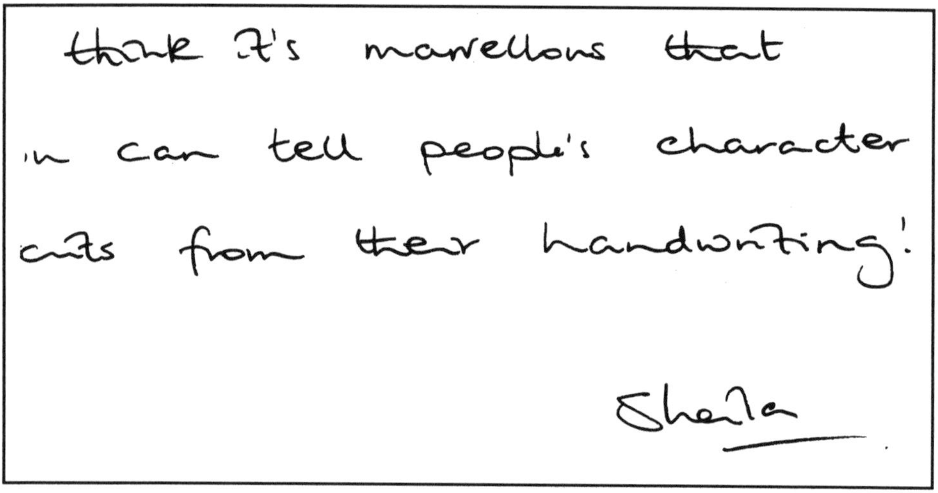

Figure 95 Spaced out signature

and self-knowledge, but the upright slant, linked i-dots and distancing of the signature from the text (soon to be discussed) suggest to me an initial scepticism about graphology!

Signatures which engulf all available space and possibly invade other script too, show *irritation at being enclosed or curbed by* petty restrictions. Conversely, note the adaptability of the writer who obligingly suits his name-size to fit a given space. Again, substitute 'me' or 'me and my family/status' to have a clear picture of the individual's attitude to confined space.

The positioning of the signature reflects the stance adopted in public. Fig. 95 shows a distancing from the subject matter and a slight desire for the writer's individuality to be noticed. Fig. 93, close to the text in circumstances not enforcing this — plenty of room on the page — shows considerable involvement with the subject matter, as does Fig. 92. The significance of a signature which retreats to the left was discussed above; such a writer is like an animal which would prefer to return to its hole and give life a miss altogether.

A signature which is placed **well to the right** of the page shows *activity and enthusiasm*, but this type of positioning will never be evident from the signing of a typed letter, which is ready 'blocked'. Spacing out, however, will take the signature in a noticeably rightward direction, showing eager intention.

Signature slant also relates to the rest of the script. When there is a sudden uplifting, the individual is self-inspired (lifted) and **ambitious**: substitute 'me and my family/status' for the signature in Fig. 96 to see ambitious zeal in which the intimate self and its needs play a very small part.

Figure 96   Rising baseline

A downslant in the signature is quite likely to be temporary, and *due to fatigue or demoralization*. In this case, the rest of the writing will also have a down-slanting baseline. When only the signature has such a base slant, 'me and my family/status' clearly cause impulses which are far from inspiring: they move towards areas of negativity (see page 54).

Me and my family

One part of the signature only may relate to the text in the ways shown. The forename represents 'me', Freud's childish *id*, first formed and least conscious part of our personality. **Contracted writing in the 'me' alone** — seen in context of the whole script — indicates *unhappiness within oneself*: there is not sufficient confidence for the 'me' signature to be written freely and openly.

Beauchataud believes that the converse, an over-mature and exaggeratedly projected forename, shows narcissism — an all-pervading love of and preoccupation with oneself.

As a general principle this attitude applies to any isolated word (usually a name) in the text. (See Fig. 43.)

Me and my family

Contraction in the surname indicates *hostility towards the spouse or family*, especially if the surname is written on a lower level than the forename, showing it to symbolize a burden.

In the signatures of unhappily married people, tension and contraction are more likely to be found in the forename, showing personal suffering, and where this is reduced to initials, they may be small or embellished with circles. Contraction, decrease in dimension or an **uneven baseline** in signatures always indicate lack of ease, though excitement of a happy kind can cause a wavy baseline.

Encircling of the signature or any part of it *shows a desire to hide*. In an irresolute signature (lacking firmness, harmony and simplicity) the writer may want to protect his image through feelings of inadequacy, but in a strong signature of good Form Level which matches the text there may be more positive reasons for wishing to hide. Encircling of the name means that the stroke surrounds, but does not cut through the signature.

Embellishment of the signature means that other, unnecessary, strokes or movements are added to the writing of the name, whether by direct connection or in the space closely surrounding it.

Heavily embellished signatures may date back to adolescence, as mentioned on page 117. Their additional strokes relate to the dreams of early youth rather than to a present-day image. If newly evolved, they must be analysed as space symbols.

Large knots and inverted letter forms show a desire to deceive, but these are not necessarily found in illegible signatures — soon to be discussed. Interpret this sign judiciously: it is a serious assessment to make.

Hooks at the beginning or ending of signatures should be treated as in **Small Signs**. To many graphologists they suggest **persistence**.

A signature which is crossed through with a straight stroke shows *intense dissatisfaction with the personal and extended selves*, with the individual's entire standing. Such a signature (see Fig. 97) placed to the left of centre and of diminished dimension, is one of the few real red flags of graphology, a warning that the writer may try to harm himself. Patricia Marne points out that a number of murderers have also crossed through their signatures. (See also Fig. 92.)

Parallel lines above and below the signature are a *sign of a go-getter*, someone with the wish to conquer or dominate, and with the strong will also associated with a single firm, long underlining stroke (see Fig. 92). The parallel line formation makes a channel for the individual to project

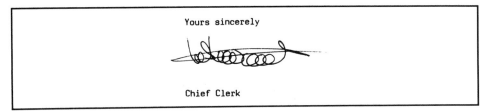

Figure 97 Signature crossed through

himself into the future; I see it as the barrel of a cannon from which force will explode.

Brief underlining (see Fig. 95) shows determination but also a *projection of will*.

Many underlinings show *frustrated will*.

Curly embellishments as an underlining indicate *showmanship*. Whether or not the writer believes in this false public persona is shown by the formation of the name itself, and the extent to which the embellishment is linked to the signature. This definition is mine, drawing together many graphological opinions which amount to this characteristic. (The signature of Elizabeth I in *What Your Handwriting Reveals* illustrates a personality who identified herself with her own publicity!) When the scroll embellishment is quite separate the writer probably takes the public image with a pinch of salt, and can use it or discard it at will.

Illegible signatures belong (according to Beauchataud) to those who have not the courage to say their own name. In terms of space symbolism this must be true, but the matter is more complex than that. We have already noted the dream signatures evolved during adolescence, which are themselves a drawing of an ideal rather than the writing of a name, and we shall find illegible signatures in the script of people who certainly do not lack courage and may show signs of will and ambition (see Figs. 94 and 96).

Those who must sign their names many times a day are *merely rubber-stamping* the statements typed above their names. The process of signing is automatic, and the name is not going to be read since it is either familiar to the recipient (as with doctors' prescriptions) or identified in type print immediately below (see Fig. 97). This does not make the signature's movements meaningless: they have, unless they are a childhood relic, evolved from regular impulses. An experienced graphologist will be wary of saying much about an illegible signature in isolation, though the small signs described in this section are standard.

Wherever possible, signatures should be treated as a part of the text, but it is inevitable that the increase in typewritten communication — meaning that the signature is the only glimpse of writing to be had — will bring about a need for the study of signatures as a separate phenomenon. For the moment, any assessment of an isolated signature must be hemmed in with provisos.

Envelopes

The addressing of an envelope represents the *public use of world space*, and is generally analysed in the same way as a sheet of writing. However, it is worth noting these variations, which can be outstanding. (See Fig. 127.)

Address placed high. This signifies idealism, but make sure that the writer was not anticipating a longer address.

Address placed low. With heavy pressure and extended downstrokes this may signify a materialistic nature, but again make sure that the correct length of address was anticipated. Entanglement would suggest bad planning.

Address placed to the left. Here the writer is reluctant to leave his home base and encounter the world. He is reserved, and does not tend to make the first move towards others.

Address placed to the right. This eager movement towards the future and other people is an extroverted gesture. If it has cramped line endings, lack of forethought and caution is shown.

Concentrated address. When the address stands isolated like an island in the sea an equally isolated character is suggested. He keeps himself to himself, shunning contact with others, and may be secretive.

Address spaced out or invasive. This shows — depending on other traits in the writing — a self-centred indifference to the needs of others, or a dominating, self-imposing will.

The need for envelopes to be clearly read may result in irregularities such as capitals throughout, typographic writing, slow speed or lack of spontaneity. A rising or falling baseline shows current optimism or despondency (see page 103).

III
Stroke and Letter Forms

British and American graphologists have been accused of paying too much attention to the minutiae of stroke and letter forms, and it is implied that this emphasis gives too limited a view — prevents them from seeing the wood for the trees. However, since their analyses are accurate and of penetrating insight it must be assumed that the practice of stroke and letter analysis is a valid form of graphology. Whereas the German school devolves upon form and rhythm, the French on superior or inferior traits and the Swiss on space symbolism, the American graphological foundation may be said to be stroke quality, and the British, letter forms.

When letter forms are taken as individual space symbols, each of the hundreds of variations which exist can be assessed in terms of space coverage and direction bias, but it would be impossible to illustrate them all. Even the eighty-four *t* formations of the American school of graphoanalysis cannot claim to be conclusive. We are returning to our search for basic and generally accepted principles relating to stroke and letter forms, and shall attempt, as several schools including the French have attempted, to establish the separate significance of strokes and of the letters they combine to form, whilst seeing them as components of the whole — jigsaw pieces in a unified picture.

But first, a further word about graphoanalysis, which is based on stroke formation and direction. This specialized and scientific method analysis was put forward in the second decade of this century by M. N. Bunker, a teacher of shorthand. Attracted by the graphology of his day, he deplored its lack of system and the disagreement which resulted. For him, the key to a system lay in the strokes of shorthand, to which each of his students seemed to impart a particular quality. Many years of research produced this theory of stroke analysis, which claims that impulses of the brain detect stroke quality and direction, and that these strokes can be found in any written language. It also claims that the same strokes are found if the pen is held by the mouth or between the toes. Bunker's system has interesting links with the findings of Robert Dilts and his Neuro-Linguistic Programming machine: it should be possible to verify the meaning of all these electrical impulses, though I have not yet been able to persuade anyone to take up the research.

Graphoanalysis involves careful measuring of the length and angle of each stroke, whereas letter form can only be recognized in terms of its deviation from the model form on which it is based. Central to both assessments is the ultimate *regularity* of these strokes or groups of strokes (letter forms), and the *pressure* with which they are created. Pressure alters the shape and appearance of the writing, but has not been discussed up to now because it is not truly an aspect of either vertical or horizontal tension, nor of space usage. It contributes to Form Level as dynamism because firm pressure is strength and vital force, but it needs a small passage of its own in this book, and I have placed it here. Before we continue with the significance of variation in stroke and letter forms, let us look at the forcefulness of their application to paper.

Whereas our language has adopted the French word *trait* to mean a characteristic, its use in French graphology is far more physical: it means the stroke or line of the writing — 'streak' would probably best combine the two interpretations. The *trait* is the groove made by the ink as the pen moves across the paper: its texture represents, according to Beauchataud, the thread we use to write with — to knit up our words. Once knitted, it creates the layout of the script.

The *trait* or groove

The *trait* or groove depends for its texture on the writing implement used, the way it is held and the pressure exercised on it. Often graphologists place considerable importance on the choice of pen, but I believe we must stop doing this: nowadays fewer people choose a nib or even bother to use a particular pen. In the days of the quill each nuance of pressure was evident, but modern fibretips and ballpoints disguise or distort it. Photocopying all but destroys the pressure aspect of writing, and in this particular area of graphology it is better to say nothing than to make a mistake because we have been deceived by appearances.

Pressure
The size of the writing point and its sharpness or bluntness affect the

appearance of pressure, so in the photocopied samples which follow this may be inaccurately conveyed. Certain aspects of pressure photocopy reasonably well, but on the whole the problem is similar to trying to

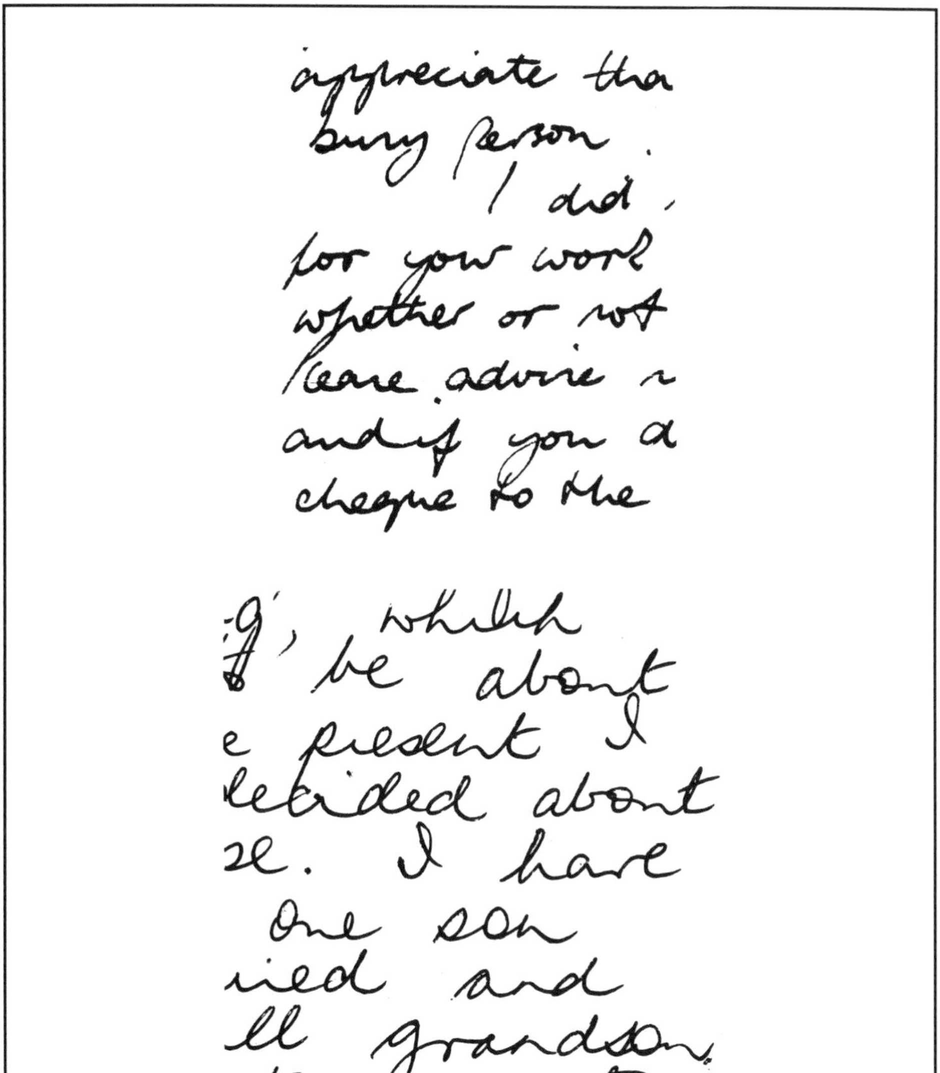

Figures 98 and 99 Deceptive pressure. *Figure 98* is light. *Figure 99* is heavy

describe the colours of a black and white photo. We cannot easily differentiate here between *heavy* and *thick* writing, or between *light* and *soft*, but bear in mind as a warning against snap judgement that crayon or chalk can produce thick writing with no pressure at all, whilst a fine pencil can be used with great force and still appear to create light writing.

Heavy pressure
With original samples there can be no doubt about this *trait* since the pressure can be felt on the underside of the paper. Klages believed that strong pressure came from 'a heavy hand or a heavy mind' and this definition is wise in its reminder that pressure can have both physical and psychological cause.

Heavy pressure is *force, applied strength*. It can deepen the groove of the writing for any of these reasons:

1. Physical health, energy, exuberance and vitality.
2. Intense application to writing as an unfamiliar occupation requiring effort.
3. Muscular pressure, which the writer probably applies to everything he does; a sign of physical or manual strength.
4. The attitude that life is a battle, that force is needed to achieve anything, that resistance must be perpetually overcome.

Check that the writing does not just *look* heavy, and do not suggest that pressure is caused by aggressiveness or sensuality (see also pasty writing) when the writer may be a gentle artist or craftsman. Thick writing, if habitual, comes from an earthy, practical nature, and may have no connection with force or will.

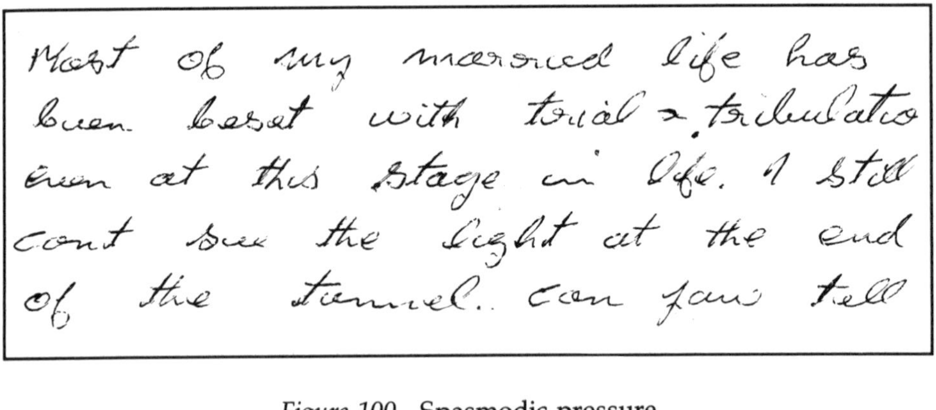

Figure 100 Spasmodic pressure

When heavy pressure ceases suddenly to be a feature of the writing, reserves of energy and vitality have been used up, and health may have deteriorated. Alternatively, life is no longer treated as a battle. Inexperienced graphologists are perhaps best advised to note *strength* in heavy pressure, and leave it at that.

Uneven pressure
First, make sure that any unevenness is the responsibility of the writer and not the pen or pencil. Secondly, differentiate at once between **spasmodic** pressure and pressure which is irregular because it is **in rhythmic relief**. Notice, too, the pattern of heavy vertical strokes which is not truly rhythmic and is discussed on page 138 under **Letter Forms**.

Spasmodic pressure (see Fig. 100 — but inadequately shown in photocopy) is a *barometer of irregular anxiety and mood*. It can indicate uncontrolled, poorly understood emotion, moodiness or irritability. At the time of writing this individual is unstable, but there may be an immediate reason: take this into account.

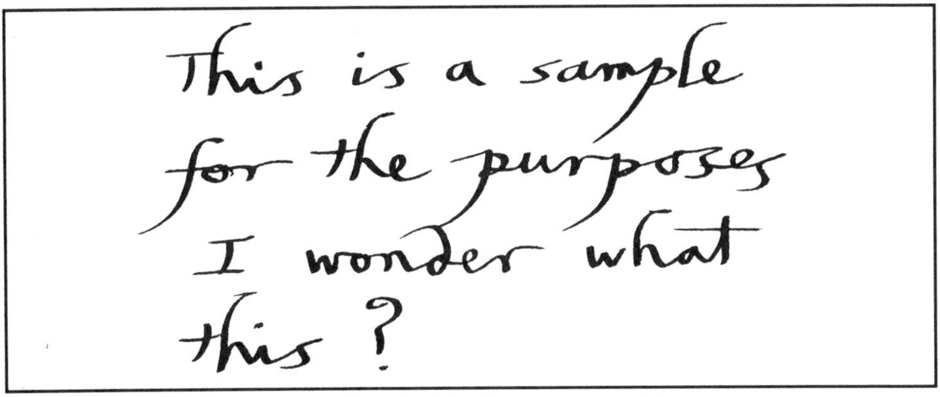

Figure 101 Italic nib — apparent uneven pressure

Rhythmic pressure does not spring from the spirit if it is deliberately contrived, as in calligraphic script. Fig. 101 shows apparent variation in pressure as part of an art form produced by a particular nib, and such pen control can be brought close to machine perfection.

Naturally rhythmic pressure (see Fig. 102) is a visible sign of the inner rhythm discussed in Form Level. It denotes *vitality of the spirit*, creativity, originality or an eagerness to get to the bottom of things. Such a person

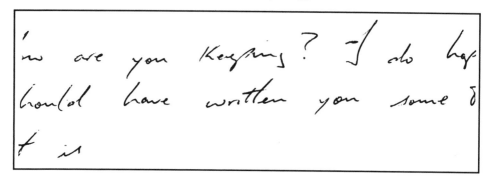

Figure 102 Rhythmic pressure

resists external influences and retains an independent mind. Rhythmic pressure must, of course, be considered in relation to other signs: we cannot say the writer has an original mind if the script shows no originality!

Even, medium pressure in writing which is neither calligraphic nor copybook cannot be a *dominant*. The writer's state of strength is not remarkable.

Light pressure

Very light writing, in which the pen seems hardly to touch the paper (see Figs. 51 and 59 — inadequately shown in photocopy), arises from any of the following causes:

1. The writer has no energy.
2. He dislikes force.
3. He is skilled enough in the writing process to produce script with a minimum of energy.
4. He is writing at great speed.

All these definitions suggest *a lack of applied force*, and this can be mental or physical in basis. If the writing used to be heavy and is now light, there has been either a withdrawal of physical energy (health) or a movement away from earthiness (living through the physical senses).

'Unearthed' people habitually use light writing: their thoughts and inspirations are of more reality to them than the concrete and tangible objects which surround them. They may have a definite fear of reality, or they may be weak of body, their agility and strength lying in the mind. Low Form Level writing whose groove is light may show impressionability. The writing of old people varies considerably in pressure and needs careful interpretation. Light writing in the teenage years calls for a sensitive approach.

Pasty writing
Not all thick writing is heavily applied. Thick, heavy writing shows *domination by the senses and earthly things*, and its writer may be materialistic, insensitive or even brutal. He has an unswervingly realistic

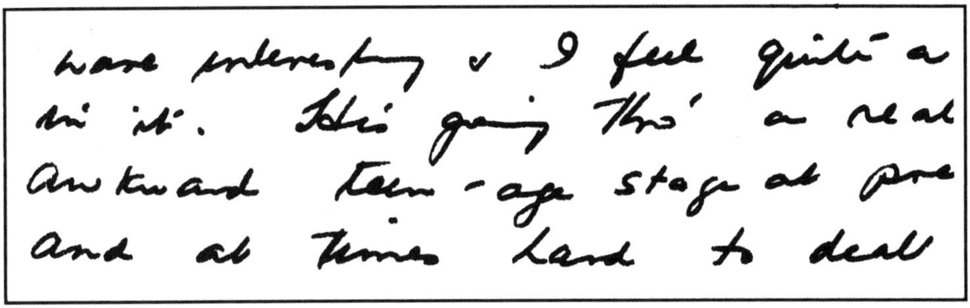

Figure 103 Pasty writing

approach to life (see Figs. 4, 87 and 99). Lighter pasty writing shows equal sensuality but more taste; a relishing of visual treats, colours, feelings and sounds, possibly at the expense of moral judgements (see Figs. 84 and 103).

Thin writing
This is the opposite of pasty writing. If the letters are well-proportioned overall (as in Fig. 104) the writer, though not necessarily sensitive or fragile of spirit, may show through his fine and even pressure a *well-established philosophy of thought and action*. Though quiet and modest, his

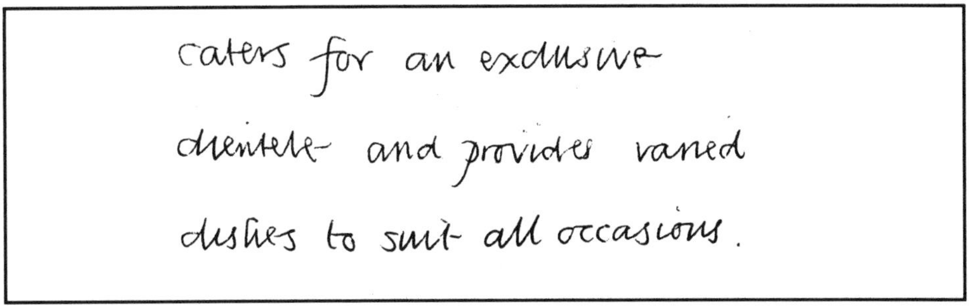

Figure 104 Thin (fine) pressure

dryness and lack of sensuality carry within them the seeds of critical or dogmatic opinion. These seeds germinate into a deliberate aversion to fun, frivolity and imagination when the letters are tall or concentrated: the writer makes a virtue of his lack of *joie de vivre* and may be boring or pedantic, a bloodless character who lives by his own rulebook (see Fig. 32).

Pressure of endings indicates *whether or not the individual projects and fulfils his desires.* The endings may be abnormally thin and sharp (*needle*) or noticeably thickened (*clubbed*). The writer is fulfilled to the extent to which his strokes are completed, and thickened strokes are not completed: they end abruptly, showing repression of passionate will in whichever zone they lie (see Figs. 52 and 55). Needle endings show will which is made manifestly clear, and sharply pointed t-bars traditionally mean irritability.

Pressure began with a warning and it ends in the same way. Always consider the writing implement and the deceptive appearance of pressure it may create!

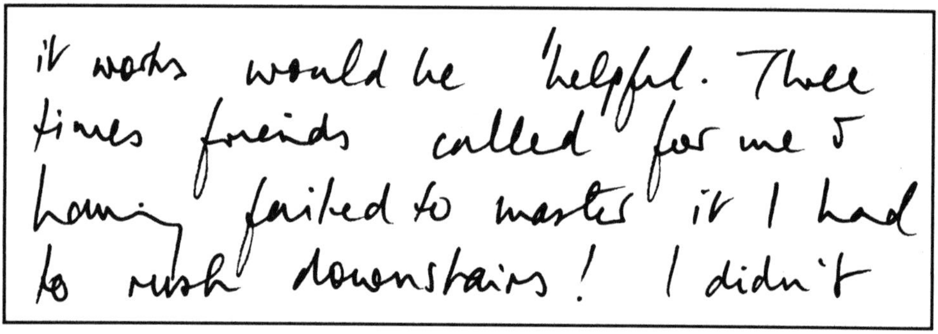

Figure 105   Needle pressure in endings

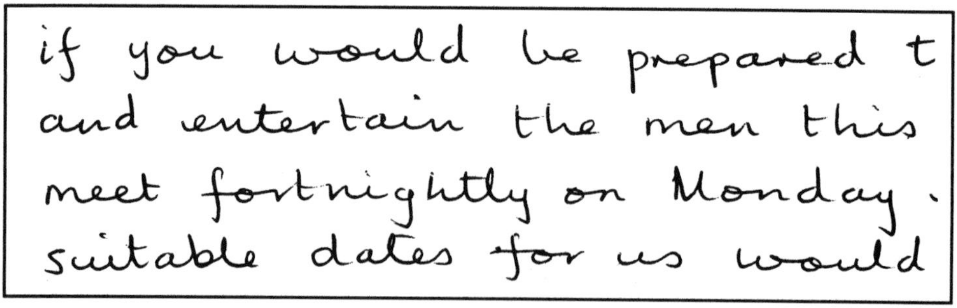

Figure 106   Clear form

Form

We come now to what can be called writing style or form. Because it

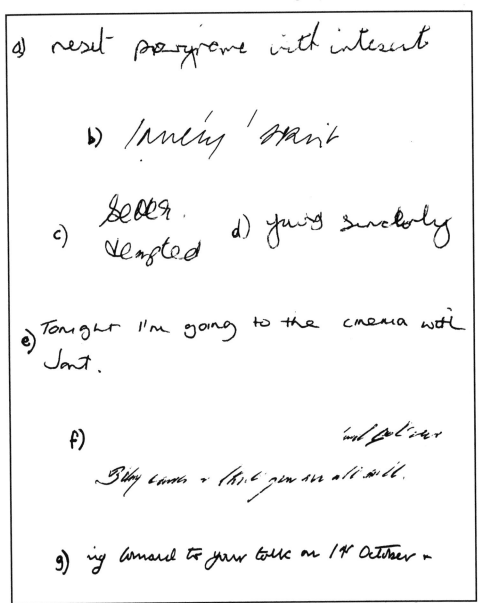

Figure 107 Illegible form: interpretations on page 144

categorizes deviation from a learned pattern of stroke or letter forms, it is to some extent a barometer of maturity, showing the aptitude of the writer's spirit in choosing, creating, imagining or organizing. Inspirational, intellectual and physical development are all mirrored, and we must not forget the detrimental effects of poor health or disability on the form of the writing. Disorganized writing (see Fig. 13) cannot be fairly subjected to any of the eye-training exercises which follow, since its strokes may not be as their writer intends them.

Clear or illegible?
Writing may be well-ordered and easy to read through the sincerity and lack of pose of its writer, but it may also be markedly clear because it *is* posed: calligraphic and copybook writing are both consciously produced art forms, and many calligraphic styles do not lack subtlety. *Clear writing is harmonious, legible, simple and uncontrived*, as in Fig. 105. It communicates effortlessly — surely the chief purpose of all writing, and shows a certain artlessness of spirit unspoiled by bitterness or sophistry.

Illegible writing is not concerned with communicating clearly. The writer sets his sights on some distant subject or goal, and what he writes is merely a means to that end. The script may be illegible through impatience or the need for immediate fulfilment, or through physical disability. In slow writing, where there seems to be no special haste and the Form Level may be poor, illegibility spells insincerity. There is an unwillingness to expose character or intention, and this form generally disturbs the reader, provoking quite justifiable hostility or disquiet.

It is extraordinary how often we guess at illegible words, using their neighbours to suggest a probable meaning. Illegibility is often in the eye of the reader.

Impersonal or personal?
Writing which shows no innovation, no deviation from established form, shows submission of individuality to ready-made principles. In copybook script (Fig. 108) the writer deliberately conforms, and lack of self-awareness shows in the contraflow movements which seem to want to break the mould, but are restrained and brought back to the taught pattern. Refer to page 34 under **Originality**.

Deviation from a taught style is caused by idiosyncratic brain impulses, which is why calligraphic writing cannot show character (refer to page 35). Originality of mind, if allowed to supersede all conventions, becomes eccentricity, and the writing of eccentrics rarely shows harmony or rhythm (see Figs. 51, 88 and 122). Bizarre deviations show bizarre tastes.

Personal handwriting is what the term suggests: a recognizable form

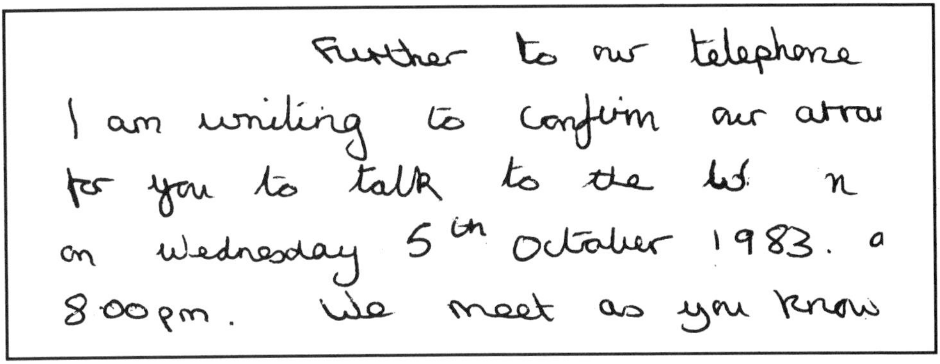
Further to our telephone
I am writing to confirm our arra
for you to talk to the W. n
on Wednesday 5th October 1983. a
8.00pm. We meet as you know

Figure 108 Copybook form

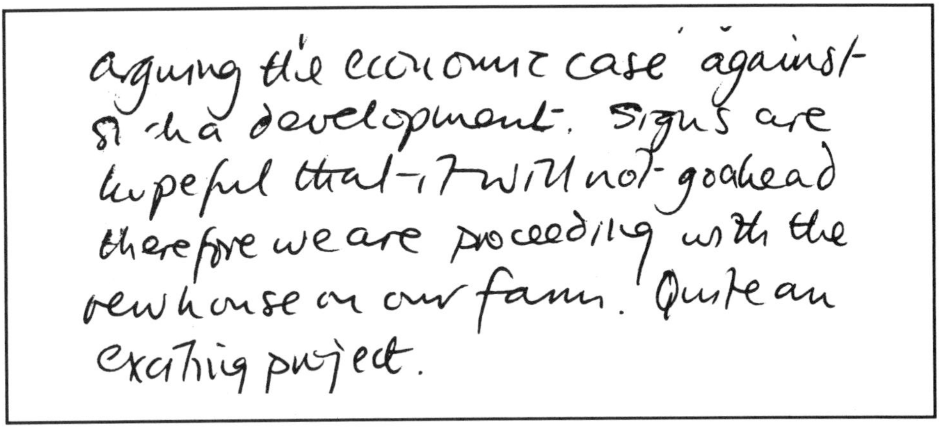
arguing the economic case against
such a development. Signs are
hopeful that it will not go ahead
therefore we are proceeding with the
new house on our farm. Quite an
exciting project.

Figure 109 Personal form

which identifies or at least reminds us of a certain writer. For writing to be personal it must have authentic originality, rather than conscious embellishments as in Fig. 113.

Simplified or amplified?
Simplified form implies that the writer has got the relevant information down on paper with a minimum of fuss. He may take short cuts in forming strokes and letters, but he does not neglect the strokes as in thread writing (Fig. 59) or illegible script. Whilst allowing idiosyncratic brain impulses to dominate he retains clarity: indeed his brain impulses are clear, concise and often backed by considerable intelligence.

Compare the personal 'I' in Figs. 110 and 111. It will be obvious that we

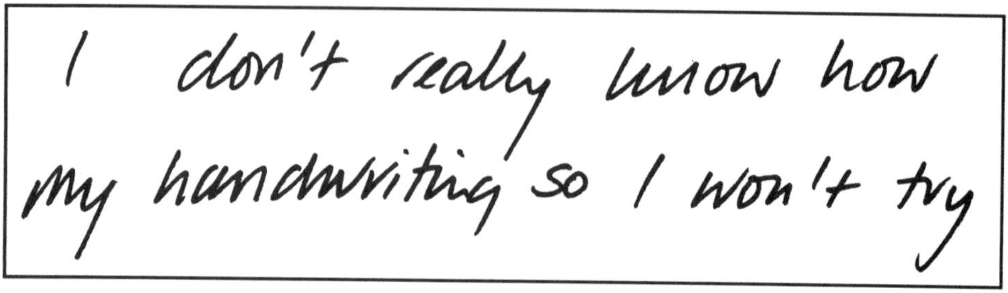

Figure 110   Simplified form

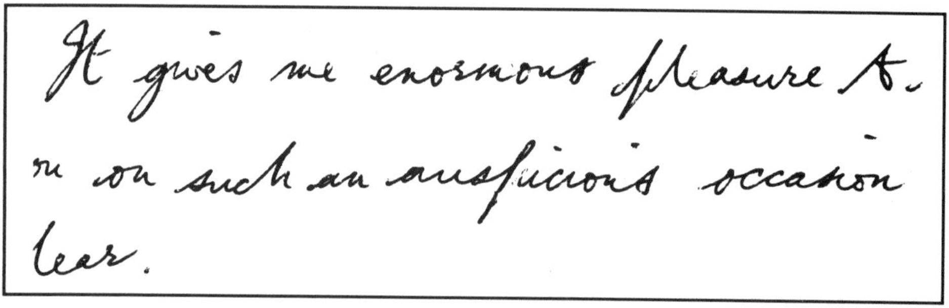

Figure 111   Amplified form

are talking about expenditure of ink and effort. (The personal 'I' shows the simple or complex way in which we view ourselves, and this was covered in *What Your Handwriting Reveals*.) Amplified writing indicates an excess of energy or vitality: sometimes overactivity to little effect is suggested. With rounded forms there may be a tendency to embellish facts, and a certain amiable folly enriches and enlivens the character, as in Fig. 111. Writers of simplified forms find time for facts: amplification means time for living.

Neglected or embellished?
Trembling, twisted and broken strokes are included in this aspect of form, which is rarely consciously negligent. If the writing is illegible that is how we describe its form, calling **neglected** only those letter forms which do not seem deliberately rushed. (Rough notes usually have spontaneity and other signs of speed.) Almost always, some *physical or mental debility* lies behind neglected form, though a faulty writing implement can give the same appearance. Tiredness or laziness, boredom or apathy should be suspected if punctuation is missing, but twisted or trembling strokes are a sign of age, illness or — especially when all else is precise — the influence

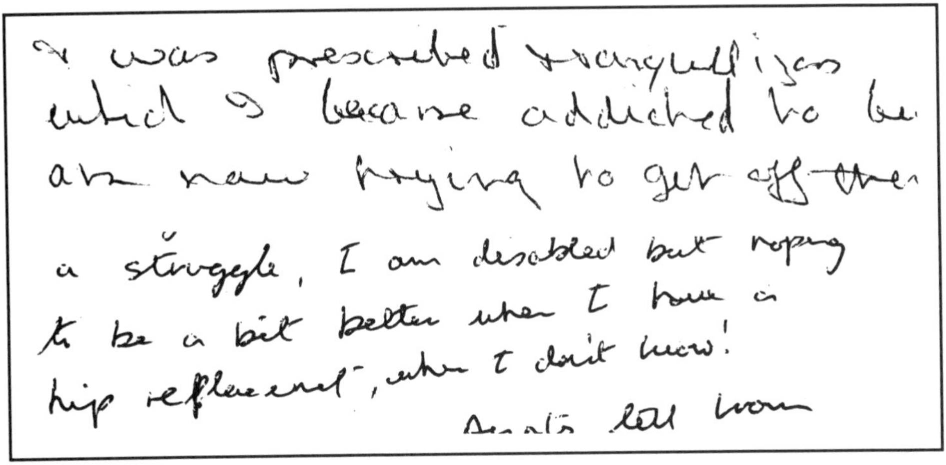

Figure 112 Neglected form

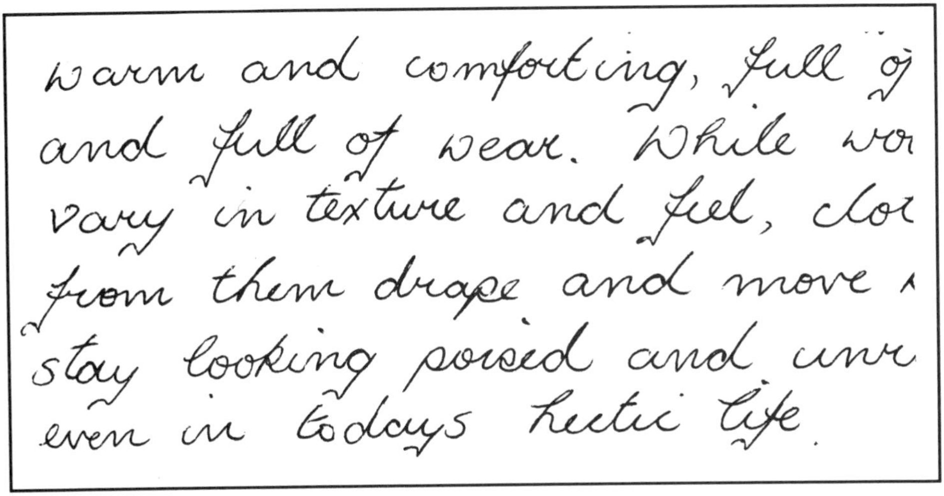

Figure 113 Embellished form

of drink or drugs. Neglected form is very difficult to interpret correctly, and the general principle above covers most causes, from the effects of writing on a train to cold, fear or complete lack of interest in the process of writing. If one zone only contains all the neglected strokes, look to pages 92–101 for likely causes.

Finally, remember our animal moving away from its hole: something is wrong with it. We may have to look at the rest of its behaviour to find out what, and it is wise to look at the rest of the writing, too. Both samples in Fig. 112 show effort — slow speed, good punctuation, retouching and legibility. (Fig. 15 shows neglect through speed.)

Embellished writing has unnecessary additions to an already complete form. Whilst this may indicate lack of taste or intelligence, a fairer general principle of interpretation is a preference for trimmings, an *interest in the appearance rather than the substance*. This is especially true if the embellishments overshadow the basic form. Vanity, pretentiousness or boastfulness are only implicit if there are other signs in the writing such as an over-large signature or capitals which attempt to underline (see Fig. 2).

Vertical or rounded?

Some writing contains a preponderance of vertical strokes, showing pressure exerted downwards:

Figure 114   Vertical form

Fig. 114 is written in pencil, with heavy pressure. All script of **vertical form** (containing a large number of vertical strokes) shows a *need to make things factual and concrete*. The writing is not always angular (see Figs. 26 and 39) and vertical form in a more mixed stroke arrangement may show an isolated gift or tendency, such as mathematical ability, which does not dominate the personality. Never guess at this gift: the writer may be an artist, sportsman or miser! Use the general principle unless other signs make you quite certain.

In very angular form, with abrupt endings and a vertical or backward slant, wide word spacing but lean letters, the writer may habitually put material or factual matters before social relationships, and have a tendency to break these off suddenly.

Rounded form — circular movement — is always associated with feeling, and the writer may be *chiefly motivated by his feelings* (see Figs. 33 and 87). Much writing is particularly in rounded form, and here as in fully rounded form the circular trait is significant in the a and o.

Open at the top — *open to higher things*. This stroke formation shows sincerity and an artless honesty, but if the script is fast or soft (without dynamism) there may be a tendency to indiscretion. (See Fig. 25.)

Open at the bottom — *open to deceit and hypocrisy*. This very rare form is considered infallible in meaning by graphologists: less certain but allied are a and o formed by two half circles, or closed at the bottom.

Ovals in a and o show *discretion* which can be taken to the point of secrecy. Trust the writer but don't expect confidences in return.
In graphoanalysis, or any system which is based on stroke analysis, each stroke, bend and curve is measured, graded according to a set scale, and the numbers of each grade counted. The value of this type of analysis — which relies less on eye training than on scrupulous examination with instruments — is shown in the next few pages.

Regularity
Regularity in writing means evenness and equality of each separate stroke, and we shall take a close look at this most fastidious aspect of graphology very shortly.

Before we do, I want to draw attention to the most neglected rule of regularity, the big 'IF' of L'Abbé Michon quoted in the first section of this book: '*If this writing is ... habitual ...*'

Regularity between samples from the same writer is by no means to be assumed. All graphologists receive letters like Figs. 115 and Fig. 47, and they warn that we may be seeing only one of several sub-personalities in the sample before us.

Fig. 115 is an extreme example of irregularity in one hand, and interpreting its meaning is not basic graphology. Suffice it to say that many people can summon up a sub-personality who writes in a different hand: the *alter ego* dismissed in adolescence as exterior and interior forces, conscious and unconscious, combined to create a unified self. Adolescent writing is seldom regular between samples, nor should it be. Maturity comes with experience, and the teenage years are for finding oneself through experience and experiment.

When samples of writing show modest irregularities between them, the

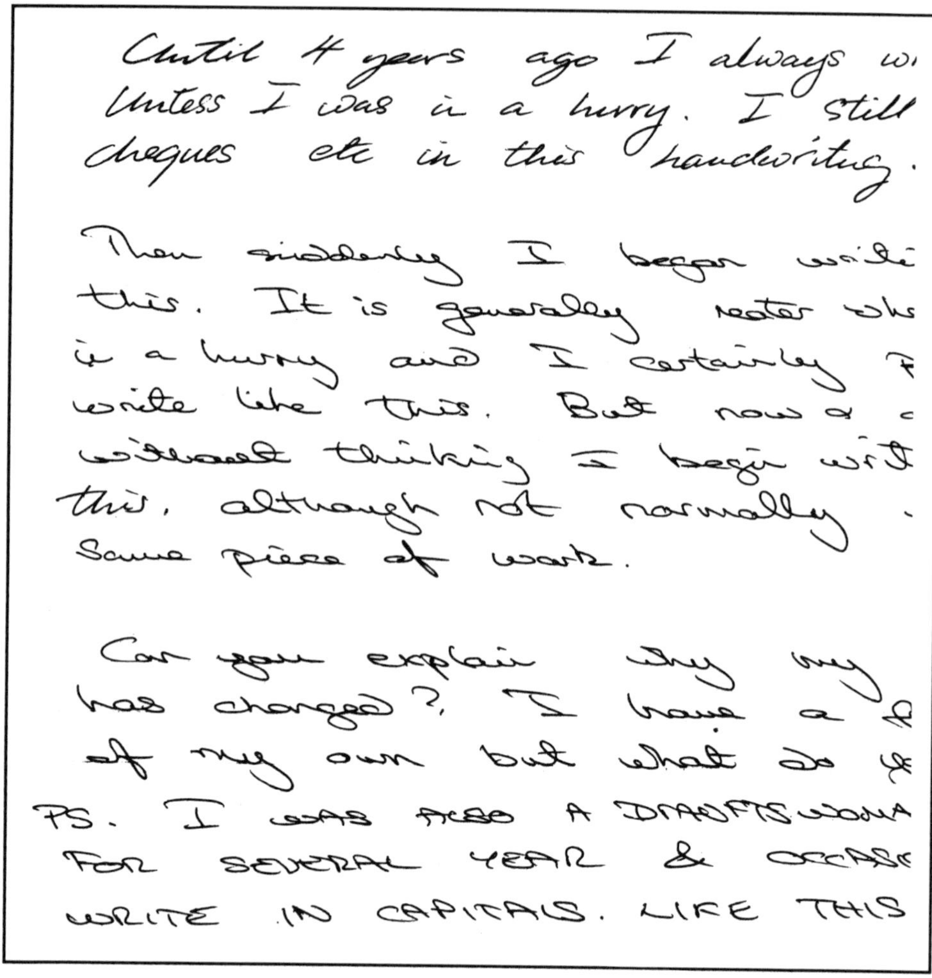
Until 4 years ago I always w
Unless I was in a hurry. I still
cheques etc in this handwriting.

Then suddenly I began writi
this. It is generally neater whe
in a hurry and I certainly
write like this. But now &
without thinking I begin writ
this, although not normally .
Same piece of work.

Can you explain why my
has changed?. I have a
of my own but what do
PS. I WAS ALSO A DRAFTSWOMA
FOR SEVERAL YEAR & OCCASI
WRITE IN CAPITALS. LIKE THIS

Figure 115 Irregularity between samples

writer is subject to swings of mood or motivation. Form quite often becomes round when an affectionate letter is being composed, contracting into angularity when facts are the subject in hand (see Fig. 116). The writing may become spaced out or dilated when the future looks bright, but held back in lean form when it threatens! Take these differences into account. They will be discussed again in Section V.

Regularity within a sample

At first glance Fig. 117 appears to be harmonious, rhythmic, spontaneous and of uniform style or form. The first three attributes of Form Level, deliberately assessed by the overall standard of the writing remain true, but the question of uniformity or *regularity* must be decided on quite a different basis.

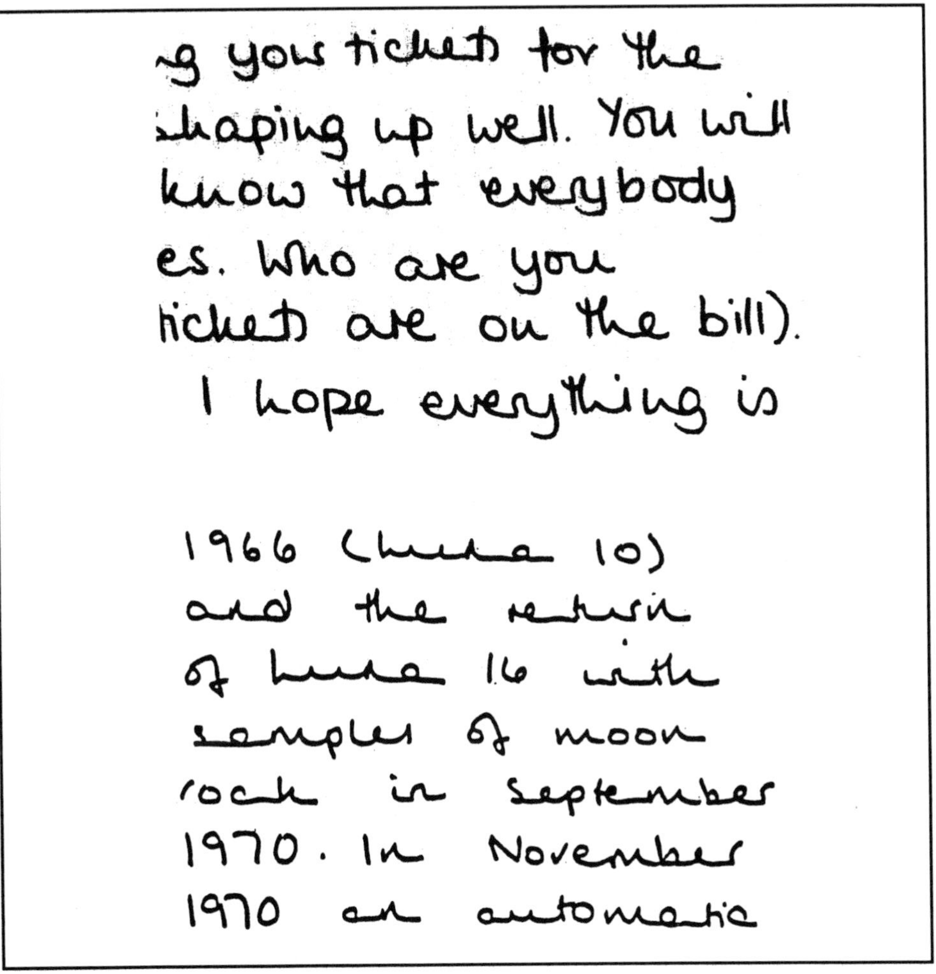

Figure 116 Irregularity between samples. Written within a few days of one another by the same hand

In deciding the degree of regularity we may have to resort to ruler and protractor, because we need to check all these strokes or letter forms:

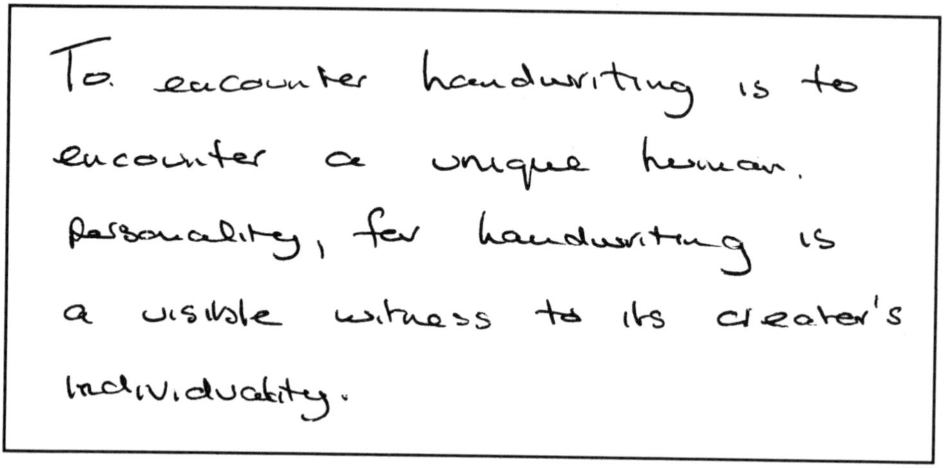

Figure 117   Slightly irregular form

Dimension (especially of middle zone)	**Height of uprights**
Speed	**Depth of downstrokes**
Word spacing	**Width of letters**
Letter spacing	**Letter form**
Slant	

If we look closely at Fig. 117, our findings will be:

Dimension. Varies in the middle zone from 1 mm (small) to 3 mm (large).
Speed. Slightly irregular, probably due to copying out the lines.
Word spacing. Varies from 5 mm to 9 mm. This is only very slightly irregular.
Letter spacing. Mainly regular, Concentration in 'visible' and 'individuality'.
Slant. Varies from left slant to vertical. Look at 'handwriting' in line 1. Graphoanalysis would measure the exact angles and code each one before adding them up.
Height of uprights. Varies from 2 mm (d in *individuality*) to 5 mm (h of *handwriting* in line 1 and f of *for*).
Depth of downstrokes. Varies from 2 mm (y of 'personality') to 4 mm.
Width of letters. Varies from 1 mm (e in 'personality', n in *individuality*) to 3 mm (u in 'human'). There are very few lean letters.
Letter form. Generally regular. t-bars and i-dots totally regular.

Generally, clear, simplified, partly rounded and with rhythmic pressure.

In Fig. 117 irregularity lies mainly in the slant, middle zone and height of uprights. These are social aspects, connected with the philosophical or inspirational zone. The writer is probably going through an unhappy period of readjustment.

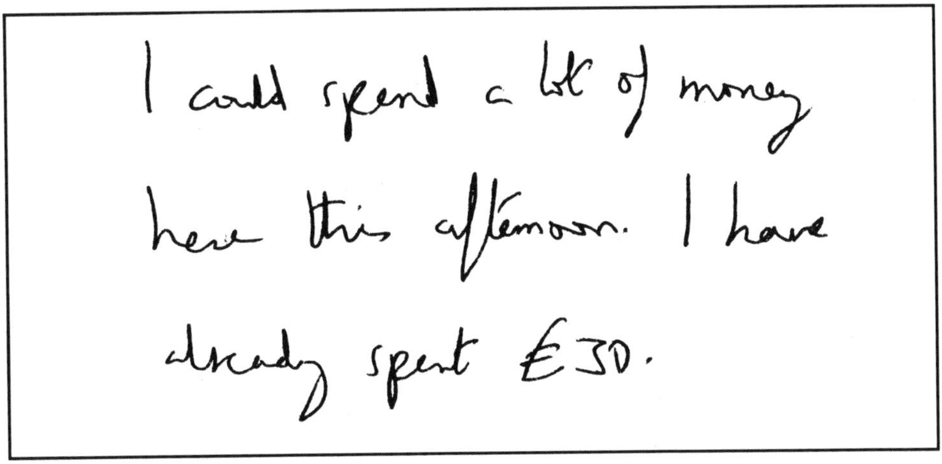

Figure 118 Very irregular writing

Fig. 118 shows the following:

Irregular dimension	Irregular height of uprights
Slightly irregular word spacing	Irregular depth of downstrokes
Irregular letter spacing	Irregular width of letters
Irregular slant	Irregular letter form (o, a, f, t, s, y, d)

The enlarged personal I is of interest in this collection of *varied and sensitive responses to life*: it has the simple awareness of a radio receiving mast.

To be added to the list above is *irregularity of signature*. Figs. 117 and 118 were both accompanied by matching signatures, irregular to the exact extent of the rest of the text, showing a good degree of self-knowledge.

This assessment of regularity cannot be completely comprehensive, and the French covering definition of regular *movement* takes the examination away from the particular to the general, where we may notice other irregularities. Do not miss these out. A discussion of regularity brings into focus the importance of looking into more than one method of analysis, since each is accurate in its own way.

Very regular writing shows a high degree of character stability, but Teillard calls its creator *mechanized man*. The regularity of calligraphic or copybook script, and the reasons behind its composition (see pages 35 and 36) demonstrate the ultimate in rigid self-control and obliteration of individual traits — traits used in both French and English senses. For the first time in this workbook we should read the words in the sample! Look at Fig. 117, quoted from *What Your Handwriting Reveals*. Writing cannot be a witness to its creator's individuality if all individuality has been carefully ironed out! The small conflicts we all experience spring from the place where the conscious and the unconscious meet in our minds, and they are part of spiritual growth and maturity. The slight irregularities of Fig. 117 and of most of the earlier samples in this book, show the mental fluctuations of a normal, healthy individual, with his own unique balance and vulnerability of impulse. This passage may explain why we do not expect — and perhaps do not even hope — ever to give full marks for **harmony**.

The assessment of regularity may prove a quick path to the heart of any disturbance in the mind, as happened when we looked at Fig. 117. It is part of the spadework of graphology, as vital in its precision as the holistic comprehension of Form Level or the visual symbolism of space and direction.

Key to illegible samples (Figure 107)
(a)   next programme with interest.
(b)   lovely skirt.
(c)   better tempted
(d)   yours sincerely
(e)   Tonight I'm going to the cinema with Janet.
(f)   got our B'day cards and that you are all well.
(g)   ...ing forward to your talk on 14th October.

IV
Typologies

The categorizing of types of writing based on types of behaviour is a natural outcome of combining a study of psychology with graphology, or of many years' experience in analysing. I confess that my own first impression sometimes takes the form of an unspoken but definite labelling, which must be forgotten at once if the writing — or the character behind it — is to be fairly described.

'Typing' handwriting is interesting and almost inevitable if a sample shows particular traits supremely well. From the eye-training exercises so far we have established a calligraphic type of writing and a copybook type, and we know that each of these implies that the writer is a certain type too. That, of course, is not the full story. Typologies never are the full story: the American sociobiologist Ernst Mayr rejects them as incompatible with evolutionary thinking and individual uniqueness. Any 'fixed, unchangeable *eidos* underlying observed variability' is for him quite out of date.

As with patterns of innate behaviour, the danger of recognizing graphological types is that analysts tend to become hooked on their own favourite version, and may tend to interpret character primarily in its terms. (An experienced graphologist looked at a sample of writing I was holding at a conference and said only, 'Thinking extrovert'. The writing was mine!) Seeing writing in terms of an overall pattern only is as bad as simply looking for small signs and interpreting them in isolation.

However, any method of analysis which presents a true reflection of character in handwriting should contribute to the final portrait. The French schools of Dr Carton, Le Senne and St Morand put writers into mental of psycho-physical groups, and a knowledge of these types still forms part of the French syllabus. It is unlikely that they will be included in a British or American syllabus. It is possible that the Psychological Types of Jung, first related to handwriting (in published form) by Ania Teillard in her *L'Ame et L'Ecriture*, may need to be understood, and although Jung's own limitations have meant that the theory of four types has not been taken up or developed by any other psychologist, we are going to look at it briefly in order to see what typologies can contribute to graphology.

Teillard, who studies under Jung for thirty years, preferred his definitions of sensation, thinking, feeling and intuitive types to those of Dr Carton — who described the four temperaments of Bilious, Nervous, Sanguine and Lymphatic — because Jung's typology embraced the unconscious as well as the conscious and thus considered the psyche in its entirety.

The four functions are thought to be as follows; they are Jung's own definitions, put forward in the last years of his life in *Man and His Symbols*:

Sensation (Sense perception) tells you that something exists.
Thinking tells you what it is.
Feeling tells you whether it is agreeable or not.
Intuition tells you whence it comes and where it is going.

Although Jung had 'no desire to give readers the impression that such pure types occur at all frequently in actual practice' — and we shall see that they do not — he generally found that in most people one of the four functions above tended to correspond with the most obvious means by which the conscious self adapted to the world. This principal or dominant function would confer a characteristic way of behaving.

Whilst acknowledging and recommending Teillard's work, I offer the following pattern of Jung's functions in handwriting as mine, based on *Psychological Types* and my own research. It does not argue with Teillard's interpretation, but I have made a few additional comments on the four basic functions, and stopped short of the extended psychology which Jung's theory included.

Introvert or Extrovert?

Jung divided his four types into introverted or extroverted aspects, making eight types in all, and Teillard finds these differently expressed in writing. We must be wary of applying these two mental attitudes, which Jung himself found too 'superficial and general', and must remember that an introverted or extroverted stance can be taken by anyone in any given situation. The extrovert stance is outward turned, expressing what is in the mind to the world, while the introverted stance looks inward and downwards into its private concerns, and does not express them. Jung based his two attitudes on the Yin-Yang symbol (see page 55), and most of us are capable of adopting either psychological opposite, depending on circumstances.

It is true that our writing may alter as we change from one to another. The extrovert attitude *expresses* — pushes out, while the introvert holds back, using and dominating less world space. Consquently, writing from an introverted mind is usually smaller and less aerated, the movements less full or expanded and often inhibited. Our earlier animal symbolism is still relevant: while one creature embraces the world and its vigorous, sociable rough and tumble, another remains withdrawn and solitary, seeming to like its inner, secret world far more than the one outside. Some of us spend our lives as lone wolves or as happy herd-members, but many of us fit into either role, making our own pattern of inward or outward turning (see Fig. 116). We must not expect, therefore, always to find a clearly extroverted or introverted attitude in writing.

We shall now look at Jung's four functions in turn, and try to establish their effects.

The Four Functions

The sensation type responds to life through his five senses, and what they do not show him to be true he tends to distrust. He is the archetypal 'Doubting Thomas', unimaginative and proud of it, who devotes himself to down-to-earth, practical activities. In handwriting this shows in the tendency to plant the words firmly into the paper. The lower zone strokes are probably heavy, pasty or enlarged, but even if they are short they will give the impression of well-planted roots. The lower zone is often dominant, but slow, heavy writing of any depth shows that sensation is a principal or auxiliary (strongly supporting) function. As in Fig. 119, there is frequently a heavy horizontal movement at the base of the middle zone — like lead weighting along the hem of a curtain.

Teillard finds introverted sensation writing to be smaller, more pasty and with a less prominent lower zone. (Remember that the introverted mind does not express itself as vigorously as the extrovert.) The summary of the appearance of the four functions in writing on page 151 may be of further help.

The thinking type responds to life through his thought processes and needs a reason for everything. He criticizes, analyses and categorizes, linking ideas and organizing them into patterns which may become rigid and set. Because he lives in his head rather than his heart he may be a cold fish, and in any case he may be ill at ease with his own emotions: he does not value feeling as a response, finding it illogical and untrustworthy.

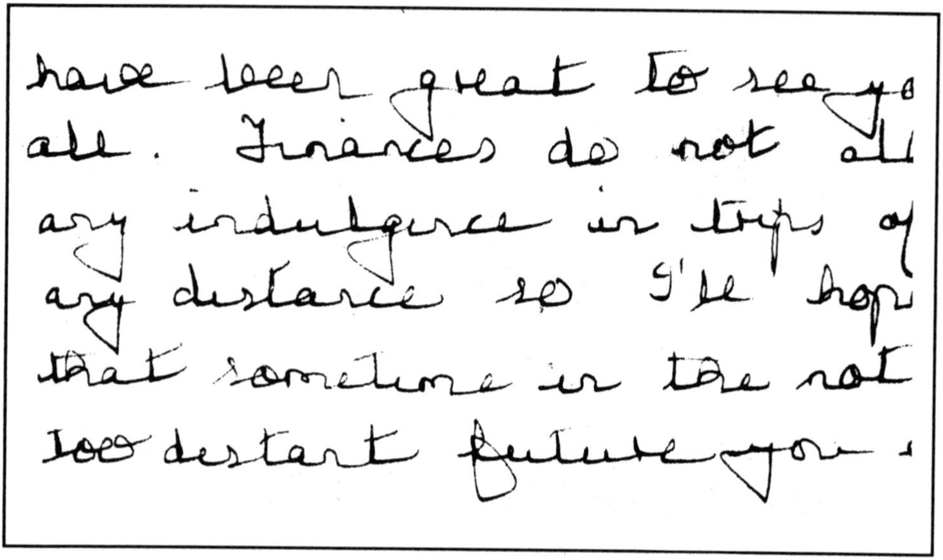

Figure 119   Principal function sensation

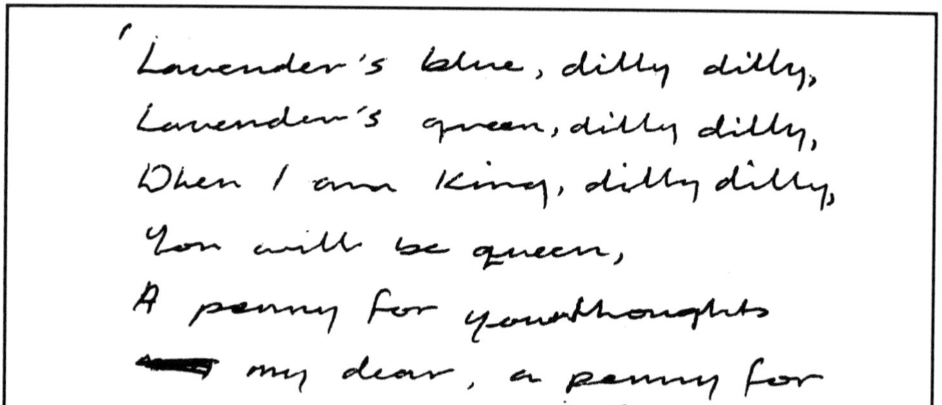

Figure 120   Principal function thinking

His writing is simplified and generally clear, often concentrated, with typographic capitals and many word or letter connections. The t-bar is frequently linked. Thinking type writing is usually well laid out and organized, with a clear, matching signature. (This type treats all things as facts, including himself.) Fig. 120 is an example of introverted thinking, and we might suppose it to be written by a middle-aged professor: in fact it comes from a 17-year-old girl.

The feeling type, on the other hand, relies chiefly on his gut reactions. Asked what he thinks about something he often replies, 'Well I *feel* that...' because that is how he most truly responds. Facts are of less interest to him than expressions of feeling, and however intelligent or academically inclined he may be, he will always be guided by an inner impulse which is not subject to any other rule than 'feeling right'.

The feeling type makes many rounded movements with his pen, and they tend to be soft and velvety and uneconomical. Like icing-sugar writing on a cake the letters bend and flow to avoid sharp angles. The script will be spaced out or dilated in an extrovert's hand, for the larger the circles the more easily the writer can express his feelings, but both extrovert and introvert tend to use medium, even pressure and a garland connection. Such writing is usually free of abrupt endings. (See Fig. 121.)

Unexpressed feeling — emotional repression — shows in rogue loops in the middle zone or in d and t uprights. (See Fig. 73.) It also produces lassos and encircling in the signature, making a picture of the problem (see Fig. 92). See also the lassos in the personal I (Fig. 1).

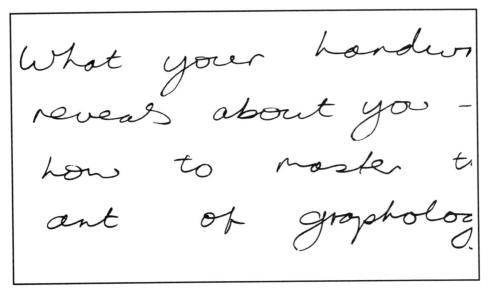

Figure 121 Principal function feeling

The intuitive type is motivated on the whole by his hunches, ideas which spring upon him seemingly from the surrounding air. Jung points out that many scientific discoveries are made in this way, though many years of research and practical experiment may lie behind them. Intuition is often a case of two and two making five, the 'intuitive leap' by-passing reason, practicality and feeling. It is shown by the extrovert in adroit business and social dealings, living by his wits and keeping one step ahead of all comers, and by the introvert as a prophet or poet. (The introvert is often a complete enigma to his neighbours, and seldom makes any attempt to explain himself: the writing of introverted intuitives and introverted sensation types may be amongst the most irregular of all forms.)

Because he does not concern himself with rational behaviour, his mind generally staying in areas of inspiration, the writing of the intuitive type visits the lower zones but briefly — unless, that is, he puts his ideas to practical purpose. Even so, the script has an appearance of being swept off the ground as this function lightens, lifts, disconnects and aerates its form.

A summary of the four functions in writing
The thinking function economizes and concentrates the writing, aligning it neatly. Capitals are typographic, the t-bars carefully crossed and often linked, and i-dots carefully placed. See Figs. 3, 14, 27, 109 and 110.

The feeling function dilates, rounds out and softens the writing, often

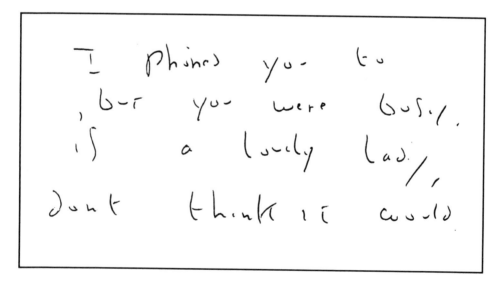

Figure 122   Principal function intuition

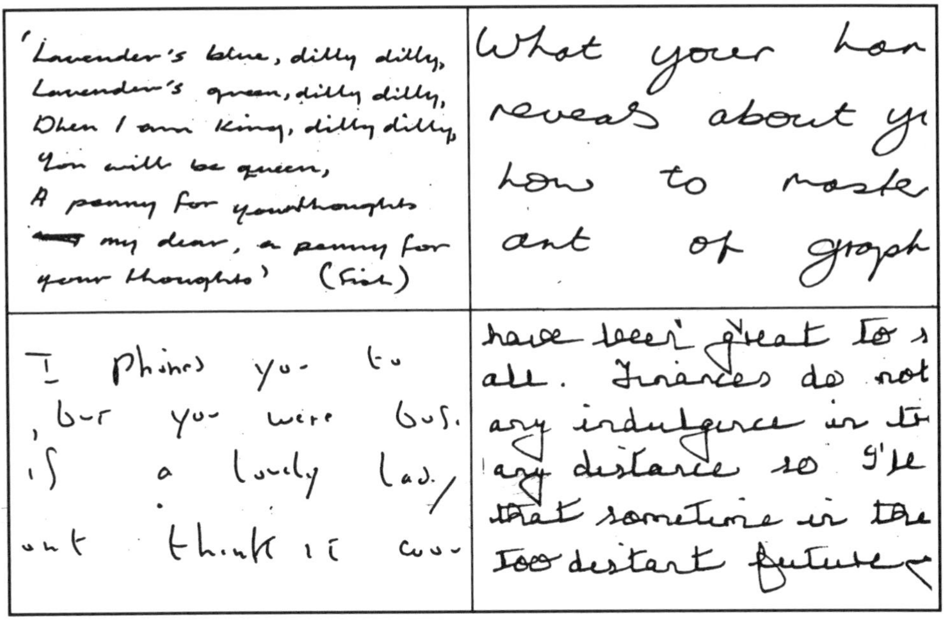

Figure 123 The four functions

enlarging it. It has a velvety and uninterrupted flow. Calm speed and spontaneity may be a feature — Fig. 19. See also Figs. 32, 60, 64 and 65.

The intuition function lightens, disconnects and aerates the writing, giving it movement but sometimes instability. See Figs. 11, 41, 51, 55 and 89.

The sensation function stabilizes or weighs down the writing, giving it a solid base. This may make it appear to move slowly, and it often is slow. The sensation function produces thick or pasty writing through heavy pressure. See Figs. 3, 23, 63, 73, 79, 94, 98, 99 and 113.

This brief introduction to Jung's Psychological Types and their functioning in handwriting is extended in Teillard's work to show their interrelationship. Jung's restrictions on which functions can work together harmoniously and consciously seem to me manifestly wrong, particularly in relation to writing, and therefore I must stop here — particularly as I have promised not to be controversial.

His insistence that sensation and intuition cannot function consciously together, or that thinking and feeling cannot similarly support one another, is not borne out either by personal observation or by noting these functions in handwriting. Though Jung's qualification *tends* to be true, it is not always so, and explains in part why his work on psychological types has not been taken up or developed since his death. The pattern which we find and note down in the bottom line of the traits chart on page 158 will probably show that any two functions can work harmoniously together. (By chance, the sample which follows it is a perfect example of Jung's principal thinking function with feeling undeveloped!)

But it is unlikely that any British graphology syllabus will teach this typology beyond the recognition of the four functions in handwriting.

The warnings about to be given apply equally to any other typology. Firstly, writing shows those functions which are *functioning consciously at the time of writing*: they may alter over days or years. Secondly, I must disagree with Teillard's statement that, 'thanks to these four functions the orientation of the individual in the world can be as complete as a geographical orientation by longitude and latitude'. I believe that any assessment of the four types can only be partially revealing. They are helpful pointers, and they suggest orientation, but that is all. I do not argue with another of Teillard's comments that, 'A large portion of the psychological troubles from which this world suffers comes from the unequal development of these four functions, which are the means of adapting to this world.' and this ancient concept, on which Jung based his work, is discussed in my book *The Four Elements*.

In a world of such amazing complexity as our own, no one typology can hope to answer all questions or solve all problems. But as yet another approach to graphology, as a contributory insight, Jung's and other typological theories have a part to play.

Dominants

A typological assessment can be a **dominant**: *one of the most noticeable and outstanding features of the writing, consistently found in all samples*. See also page 155. There is some disagreement as to whether a small sign can be dominant, and a good test is to decide whether the trait you have in mind can be seen at a yard's distance. We are talking about overall movements or patterns in the writing.

People with absolutely no knowledge of graphology at all can pick out dominant traits in writing, in fact they may be better at it than those trained to analyse the various movements, because a fresh and unprejudiced eye is needed. Graphologists who give instant assessments are picking out and commenting on dominants, and there is no harm in this so long as they do not pretend to be giving a full and considered analysis. However, they must be quite sure that they are right in their interpretation, and learner graphologists are safer sticking to the general principle of that dominant than trying to relate it to the whole character.

This work book has emphasized many times that any system of graphology which produces accurate character assessments is a valid one, and it is obvious that a continuously enquiring approach to methods of analysing must produce growth to include all known systems in this book. New ones, including computerized readouts, have come quietly into being, but other more established methods have been excluded too, partly because their practitioners do not like their systems to be handled superficially or mixed with others. Variety of approach is healthy and stimulating, and providing all include compassion, scrupulous integrity and confidentiality, and remain free of the impulse to make moral judgements, the science of graphology can only benefit from their diversity.

V
Making an Analysis

The burden of responsibility involved in summing up the nature and behaviour of another individual may be outweighed by the sheer technical difficulty of converting a list of character traits into a fluent portrait!

There is no infallible method which can be applied to this, the graphologist's ultimate task, but there are two vital attitudes which must both come into play. They are perhaps best likened to the functions of the left and right hemispheres of the brain, the first of which specializes in analytical or reasoning work, while the second picks up sensory impressions. We *must* be careful and accurate, checking constantly that no feature, no piece of the jigsaw, has been left out, and yet we *must* also look at the whole picture, at the individual emerging from the left into world space. A first sensitive glance at this lone entity as it creeps or bounds like an animal before our eyes, or — to use another image — makes its stage debut from the wings, should prevent us from over-using our analytical faculties.

Both viewpoints are vital. It is true that some graphologists receive striking impressions which may seem to cut out the need for boring spadework, but the resulting portrait will not be complete. Several stages of checking are necessary during the making of the analysis, but so, too, are the moments of standing well back from the page in order, as Klages suggests, to look at the face instead of its features.

The following suggestions are based on the experience of many practising graphologists. They belong to no one school, and the trait charts used in the early stages of assessment contain ideas drawn from various graphological traditions.

1. Preliminaries

Before making any analysis at all, it is essential to make sure that the exercise itself is valid. The following questions have to be asked and answered.

(a) Sex? You will not be able to guess this, because the mental sex may not be the physical one. Never be tempted to guess: being wrong will make all your other assessments seem suspect.

(b) Age? This cannot be guessed, either. You will need to know if the writer falls into the category of teenager, under 30, middle age, late middle age or post retirement.

(c) The purpose of the analysis? A great deal of time and energy can be wasted if a full portrait is not required.

(d) The country where writing was learned? This may be significant, especially if another alphabet was originally used.

(e) Left- or right-handed?

(f) Is the writing habitual? It is astonishing how often the answer to this is *no*. Ask for more samples.

(g) Does the writer have any physical disability, chronic or temporary, especially in the writing arm or wrist?

(h) Are there any unusual circumstances connected with the writing of the sample? Position, pen, alcohol?

If you suspect that there is some kind of motor disturbance, ask more questions, as you may make rash or wrong assessments. Alcohol can affect the rhythm of the writing for more than twenty-four hours afterwards, as can typing.

The need for these questions to be answered puts the whole exercise on to a sober footing, and tends to inspire trust in the graphologist.

2. The First Impression

The first look must be receptive rather than analytical, and I always revert to the animal symbolism so often used in this workbook. No more than a few seconds should be needed to do this: we are approaching the writing from a distance and before long we shall be close enough to notice all kinds of features and details: delay that stage! The first impression may suggest a level of Form, but that is not the point of the exercise, and the Form Level will be looked at in depth later on as a stage in analysis. This is a glance at the face, at the whole, and it must be subjective — a personal view not necessarily shared with others.

3. Dominants

The next stage allows us to determine consistently found or *dominant* features of the writing. They stand forth when the page is held at arm's length and should be noted straight away, in any order. They probably do represent some of the most powerful impulses of the personality behind the writing, and as such, a quick look at the dominants is a valid if superficial form of graphology. But it is not an analysis, and this should always be stated. A quick look at the dominants is the basis of 'fairground' analysis, and it cannot paint a full or accurate portrait. Judiciously done, however, it can prove an effective appetite-whetter for the subject, and has led many people to appreciate the possibilities of full analysis.

Part 1 of The British Institute's accrediting examination requires that you select dominants, secondary movements and miscellaneous movements. Unless there is some standardized agreement on these three groups of movements, the analytic procedure cannot be said to be scientific. It is vital that the characteristics chosen be unequivocably evident. In at least one school of graphological method, dominants are invariably chosen from a set list, e.g. size, slant, spacing, baseline, etc. I am still of the opinion that many other handwriting traits, e.g. rightward tendencies, can be a dominant feature of a script. It is expected that examination candidates will choose between five and eight dominants; those chosen will affect the balance of the final portrait.

4. Secondary Movements

These traits and patterns are less obvious traits than the dominants, and are chosen after a more careful inspection and often after measurement. What categorizes them as secondary movements rather than dominants or miscellaneous movements is that they cannot be said to be noticeable at arm's length but are observable throughout the script because they appear frequently and consistently.

5. Miscellaneous Movements

These are traits which occur minimally in the writing, such as retouching or *occasional* variation in letter form or in the *occasional* signature. If retouching is a consistent and regular feature of the writing then it is classified as a secondary movement.

6. Form Level

The six aspects of Form Level need to be considered next, and the charts which follow give some idea of how this can be done. Appraisal can be quick and the assessment approximate, but it is important to understand

CHART OF TRAITS (read from left to right)

GIVEN DATA	Name or ref.no.	Age: Sex:	Purpose of analysis:		Country writing learned?	Left-handed?	Is sample habitual?	Physical disability?	Any unusual circumstances?	
FIRST IMPRESSIONS				DOMINANTS						
HARMONY	Excellent	Generally harmonious	Slightly inharmonious	Inharmonious	ORIGINALITY	Very original	Some originality	Copybook	Pseudo-copybook	Calligraphic
ORGANIZATION	Organized	Fairly organized	Disorganized	Unorganized	SPONTANEITY	Spontaneous	Slightly inhibited	Calm	Over-spontaneous	Inhibited
DYNAMISM	Dynamism	Resolute	Low dynamism	Inhibited dynamism	RHYTHM	Rhythmic (lively)	Rhythmic but irregular	Mixed	Rhythm stilled	Irregular Uncoordinated
MARGINS	Typographic	Wide left	Wide right	Irregular on page	Invading	Exaggerated	Decreasing	Increasing	Irregular between samples	Other
WORD SPACING	Wide	Narrow	Average	Irregular	DIMENSION	Average	Large	Small	Increasing (trumpet)	Decreasing
HORIZONTAL TENSION	Spaced-out letters	Lean letters	Roughly equal height and width	Irregular	Concentrated script	Concentrated words	Aerated writing	Aerated words		
SLANT	Upright	Generally upright	Right (forward)	Slightly to right	Left (backward)	Slightly left	Mixed slant	Irregular		
CONTINUITY (Connection)	Very connected	Hyper-connected	Connected	Mixed connection	Partly connected	Disconnected (light)	Disconnected (heavy, pasty)	Broken	Initial strokes	Capitals throughout
FORM OF CONNECTION	Rounded	Garland	Arcade	Mixed (wavy line)	Mixed	Thread	Copybook			
SPEED	Slow for a reason	Slow	Calm	Accelerated	Rapid	Thread	Irregular	Resting dots	In text	After signature
LEFTWARD TENDENCIES	Oval	Lassos	Downstrokes	Middle zone	Lower zone	Upper zone	Left with left tendencies	Left tendencies in signature	Other	No left tendencies

CHART OF TRAITS (read from left to right)

MIDDLE ZONE	Relatively large	Relatively small	Angular	Rounded	Other	**UPPER ZONE**	Relatively large	Undersized	Detached strokes	Repressed
LOWER ZONE	Enlarged (extended)	Undersized	Clubbed understrokes	Deformed (distorted)	Repressed	**ENTANGLE-MENT**	Considerable entanglement	Occasional entanglement	Entanglement avoided	Deep line spacing
BASELINES	Rising	Falling	Tiled	Lined paper	Wavy	Mixed	Other			
SMALL SIGNS (Beginnings & endings)	Initial (cautionary) strokes	Hooks at beginning	Hooks at end	Abrupt endings	Horizontal endings	Upward curves	Downward curves	Plunging endings		
SMALL SIGNS (t-bars)	t-bars consistently crossed	To left / To right	Linked	Bowed	High / Low	Diversity of form	t-bars omitted	Over-large capitals	Small capitals	Other
SMALL SIGNS (i-dots and punctuation)	Regular i-dots	Close i-dots	i-dots frequently omitted	Other	No punctuation deliberate	No punctuation	Careful punctuation	Excessive punctuation	Excessive punctuation in good F.L.	Retouching
SIGNATURES	Harmony with text	Inharmonious with text	Larger than text	Smaller than text	To the far left	To the far right	Spaced out (fully)	Concentrated (fully)	Contracted forename	Contracted surname
SIGNATURES	Embellished	Encircled	Slashed through	Forename initials only	Rising / Falling	**ENVELOPE**		High / Low	Left / Right	Concen-trated / Spaced out
PRESSURE	Light	Heavy	Spasmodic	Rhythmic	Pasty	Thin / Fine	Needle	Calligraphic	Pressure in lower zone	Clubbed
FORM	Illegible / Partly illegible	Clear / Mainly clear	Personal	Copy-book / Calligraphic	Simpli-fied / Ampli-fied	Neglected (broken)	Embellished	Vertical form	a or o open at top	Ovals in top of a or o
REGULARITY	Irregular between samples	Irregular dimension	Irregular word spacing	Irregular letter spacing	Irregular slant	Irregular height of uprights	Irregular depth of downstrokes	Irregular letter width	Irregular letter form	Irregular speed
REGULARITY	or slightly irregular	or slightly (measured)	or slightly (measured)	or slightly (measured)	or slightly (measured)	or slightly (measured)	or slightly (measured)	or slightly (measured)	or slightly irregular	or slightly irregular
TYPOLOGY	Sensation	Feeling	Thinking	Intuition						

the principles behind these qualities. The more positive ratings are to the left of each aspect, the weaker to the right, so a visual picture will emerge. How you assess or grade the Form Level is a matter of choice and personal functioning — we too are affected by our psychological typing — and is also connected with our training: as a teacher I find it easy to settle on a point somewhere between D plus and A minus! Remember that the Form Level is affected by circumstances, an unforgettable example being rough notes. The gap between the given grade and 'excellence' contains the writer's nature, and these will emerge with clarity during the next stage of the analyses. I call these the *Achilles' heels* of the character, and I always spell them out. Knowing about them can alter the course of a life task.

7. Traits
It may sound harsh, but until each of the 200 traits on the chart is understood, analysing is going to be hard and slow. Understanding the general principle behind each of them means that as you progress through the chart, ticking or circling each relevant trait as on pp. 164–5, a vivid linking and grouping process takes place in the mind, increasing and strengthening with experience. This is well worth aiming for: it is the two-and-two-makes-five factor, and intuition may be the correct word for it although it is based on completely diagnosable facts. Thorough understanding of principle avoids the type of portrait in which contradictory statements stand baldly alongside one another with no attempt at synthesis (e.g. 'A warm, affectionate nature. Irritable'). This is one of the drawbacks of computerized analysis.

A Sample Analysis

We are going to return to the beginning of this section and work through the writing of one individual, an 18-year-old boy. (See Figs. 124–7.) The charts which follow are marked appropriately, but first we must look carefully at the project we are embarking on, using the numbered stages already discussed.

1. Preliminaries
These essential points are answered in the top line of the chart. The unusual circumstances are that Angus was asked to write his letter of application for a job on a piece of paper smaller than he would normally choose to use, and to fill only one side. To have a more real impression of his use of space, I have included two other samples and the envelope for the letter of application.

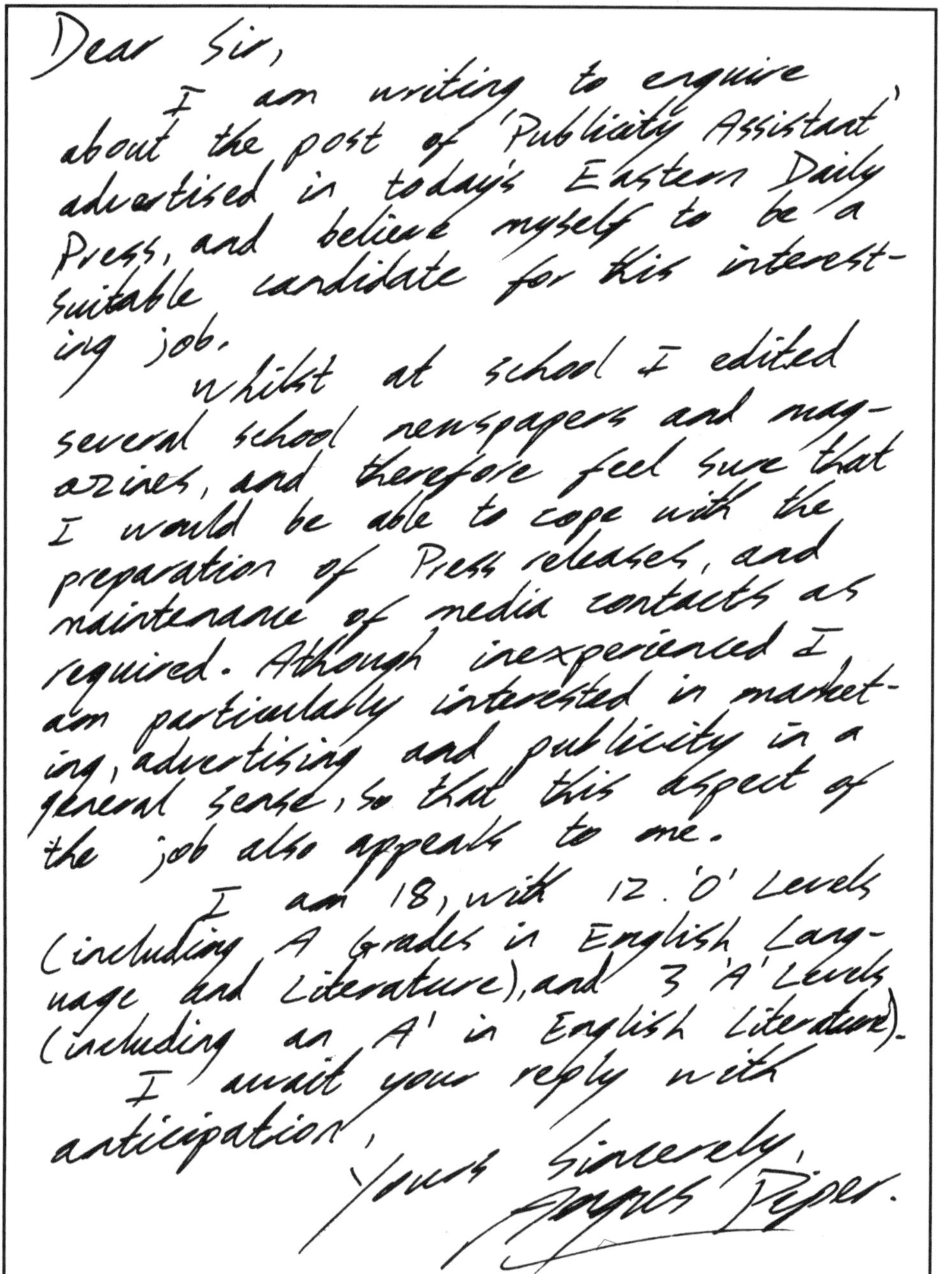

Dear Sir,

I am writing to enquire about the post of 'Publicity Assistant' advertised in today's Eastern Daily Press, and believe myself to be a suitable candidate for this interesting job.

Whilst at school I edited several school newspapers and magazines, and therefore feel sure that I would be able to cope with the preparation of Press releases, and maintenance of media contacts as required. Although inexperienced I am particularly interested in marketing, advertising and publicity in a general sense, so that this aspect of the job also appeals to me.

I am 18, with 12 'O' Levels (including A grades in English Language and Literature), and 3 'A' Levels (including an 'A' in English Literature).

I await your reply with anticipation,

Yours sincerely,
Jacques Piper.

Figure 124 Letter of job application

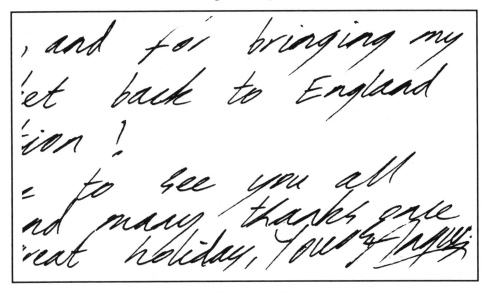

Figure 125 Sample on large paper

It is always wise to collect as many samples as possible. They act as a confirmation of frequently repeated traits, but also warn that writing does vary from sample to sample.

2. The First Impression

My first impression is that this is distinctive writing, to be recognized as *belonging to Angus* as the envelope lies six feet away on the door mat! To a stranger it is equally distinctive: the first impression may be 'Wow!' swiftly followed by an immediate subjective colouring of personal feeling.

The writer is stamping his character on our awareness, and that in itself may be considered an aggressive act.

Since our eyes are now beginning to look at specific signs in the writing we must move on, but we shall return to this first impression, which will be found to contain a curious anomaly.

3. Dominants

What makes Angus' writing so striking? I find its dominant features to be the consistent rightward slant, dynamism and dimension, the apparent overall regularity, the almost invasive layout (very small margins) and the degree of attention, to be noted even at a distance.

These dominants are found in all the samples, and in themselves create

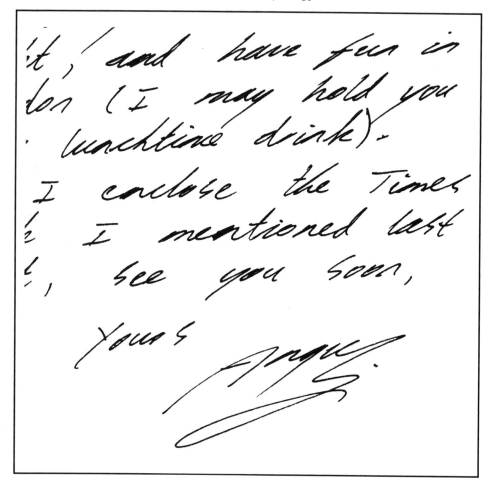

Figure 126 Sample on small paper

a certain picture. Since it is by no means the whole picture we are not going to sum it up at this point, but when the analysis or portrait is complete it may be interesting to see to what extent the dominant features gave a true overall impression.

4. Form Level

The circles marked on the traits chart are approximate, and are placed according to the general level of all the samples. If we take Fig. 124, the sample submitted for analysis, it may rate slightly less than the B+ I find

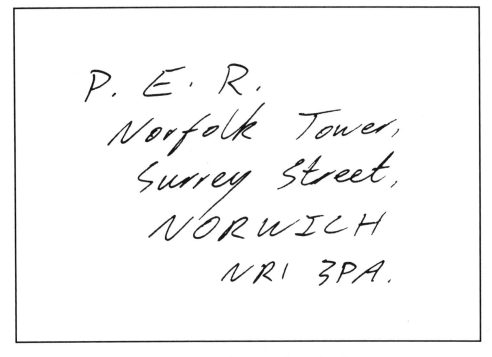

Figure 127 Envelope of job applications

fair overall, but the other samples might through their more harmonious layout rate slightly higher than B+. This is not meant to be an exact appraisal and certainly not a judgement of character, but a simple example of how to establish a Form Level.

5. Traits

It is essential to work carefully through this process, which can take an hour if regularity has to be measured. Signs or repeated features which are not listed can be added in the blank squares, and it is naturally more precise to add qualifying adjectives such as *slightly* or *very*. I sometimes add the word *transitional* if it seems that the letter form is in a state of change, and this could apply to the personal I as seen in the envelope sample. But this particular trait is not so strongly marked as to be truly transitional.

We are looking chiefly at Fig. 124 because we have been asked to analyse it from the point of view of job selection, and the circles relate to that sample. The added comment *embellished underlining* is a reminder to

CHART OF TRAITS (read from left to right)

GIVEN DATA	Name or ref.no. A.Piper	Age: 18 Sex: m	Purpose of analysis: General/job		Country writing learned? U.K.	Left-handed? No	Is sample habitual? No	Physical disability? No	Any unusual circumstances? Smaller paper than is liked.	
FIRST IMPRESSIONS	Personal, arresting, slightly aggressive			**DOMINANTS**	**Right slant**	**Dynamism**	**Dimension**	**Apparent regularity**	**Margins layout**	**Degree of attention**
HARMONY	Excellent	Generally harmonious	Slightly inharmonious (circled)	Inharmonious	**ORIGINALITY**	Very original	Some originality (circled)	Copybook	Pseudo-copybook (circled)	Calligraphic
ORGANIZATION	Organized (circled)	Fairly organized	Disorganized	Unorganized	**SPONTANEITY**	Spontaneous	Slightly inhibited (circled)	Calm	Over-spontaneous	Inhibited
DYNAMISM	Dynamic (circled)	Resolute	Low dynamism	Inhibited dynamism	**RHYTHM**	Rhythmic (lively)	Rhythmic but irregular (circled)	Mixed	Rhythm stilled	Irregular Uncoordinated
MARGINS	Typographic (circled)	Wide left	Wide right	Irregular on page	Invading (circled)	Exaggerated	Decreasing	Increasing	Irregular between samples	Other narrow (circled)
WORD SPACING	Wide	Narrow	Average (circled)	Irregular	**DIMENSION**	Large (circled)	Decreasing	Small	Increasing (trumpet)	Decreasing
HORIZONTAL TENSION	Spaced-out letters	Lean letters (circled)	Roughly equal height and width	Irregular	Concentrated script (circled)	Concentrated words	Aerated writing	Aerated words		
SLANT	Upright	Generally upright	Right (forward) (circled)	Slightly to right	Left (backward)	Slightly left	Mixed slant	Irregular		
CONTINUITY (Connection)	Very connected	Hyper-connected	Connected	Mixed connection	Partly connected (circled)	Disconnected (light)	Disconnected (heavy, pasty)	Broken	Initial strokes	Capitals throughout
FORM OF CONNECTION	Rounded	Garland	Arcade (circled)	Mixed (wavy line)	Mixed	Thread	Copybook			
SPEED	Slow for a reason	Slow	Calm	Accelerated (circled)	Rapid	Thread	Irregular	Resting dots	In text	After signature (circled)
LEFTWARD TENDENCIES	Ovals	Lassos	Downstrokes	Middle zone	Lower zone	Upper zone	Left with left tendencies	Left tendencies in signature	Other	No left tendencies (circled)

CHART OF TRAITS (read from left to right)

MIDDLE ZONE	Relatively large	Relatively small	Angular	Rounded	Other	UPPER ZONE	Relatively large	Undersized	Detached strokes	Repressed
LOWER ZONE	Enlarged (extended)	Undersized	Clubbed understrokes	Deformed (distorted)	Repressed	ENTANGLE-MENT	Considerable entanglement	Occasional entanglement	Entanglement avoided	Deep line spacing
BASELINES	Rising	Falling	Tiled	Lined paper	Wavy	Mixed	Other			
SMALL SIGNS (Beginnings & endings)	Initial (cautionary) strokes	Hooks at beginning	Hooks at end	Abrupt endings	Horizontal endings	Upward curves	Downward curves	Plunging endings		
SMALL SIGNS (t-bars)	t-bars consistently crossed	To left / To right	Linked	Bowed	High / Low	Diversity of form	t-bars omitted	Over-large capitals	Small capitals	Other / Typographic
SMALL SIGNS (i-dots and punctuation)	Regular i-dots	Close i-dots	i-dots frequently omitted	Other / Sometimes moving	No punctuation deliberate	No punctuation	Careful punctuation	Excessive punctuation	Excessive punctuation in good F.L.	Retouching
SIGNATURES	Harmony with text	Inharmonious with text	Larger than text	Smaller than text	To the far left	To the far right	Spaced out (fully)	Concentrated (fully)	Contracted forename	Contracted surname
SIGNATURES	Embellished	Encircled	Slashed through	Forename initials only	Rising / Falling	Embellished / Underlining	ENVELOPE	High / Low	Left / Right	Concentrated
PRESSURE	Light	Heavy	Spasmodic	Rhythmic	SLIGHTLY (Pasty) / Amplified	Thin / Fine	Needle	Calligraphic	Pressure in lower zone	Clubbed
FORM	Illegible / Partly illegible	Clear / Mainly clear	Personal	Pseudo-Copy / Book / Calligraphic	Simplified	Neglected (broken)	Embellished	Vertical form	a or o open at top	Ovals in top of a or o
REGULARITY	Irregular between samples	Irregular dimension	Irregular word spacing	Irregular letter spacing	Irregular slant	Irregular height of uprights	Irregular depth of downstrokes	Irregular letter width	Irregular letter form	Irregular speed
REGULARITY	or slightly irregular	or slightly (measured)	or slightly (measured)	or slightly (measured)	or slightly (measured)	or slightly (measured)	or slightly (measured)	or slightly (measured)	or slightly irregular	or slightly irregular
TYPOLOGY	Sensation	Feeling	Thinking	Intuition						

deal with that complex addition, but it does not fully exist in the job application letter.

As we progress through the trait chart a further picture emerges, and when it is complete we can draw our first rough sketch of the character behind the writing. So now we move on to stage 6.

6. The First Rough Sketch

Some graphology books suggest ways of establishing character by looking for character traits — determination, accuracy, friendliness and so on. This can certainly be done, and it may turn out to be your way of analysing, but the thorough method we are using is less fallible in that we are looking at what *is* there rather than for what *may be* there. To this end we are going to make a rough sketch of what we have found, and then look through the trait chart once more to see what we have left out.

We have heard that certain groups of signs suggest a character tendency, and sometimes the finding of one of these signs does make us start an immediate search for the others in its group. For example a falling baseline indicates current debility (tiredness) or demoralization, and this will be borne out by disorganization, low, detached or missing t-bars and light pressure. A falling baseline with disorganization and light pressure but precisely crossed t-bars (see Figs. 48 and 80) shows physical, not mental tiredness.

Now the moment the group of signs above was mentioned, I found it necessary to qualify the relationship within it. The subtleties of sign-relating may be unique to each sample, and therefore it is not necessarily wise to set out clear groupings. We might find that a grouping existed in apparently full and equal measure but was actually counterbalanced by another sign. If the traits and overall appearances noted in the charts are fully learned, their general principles can be grouped in a much fairer way as each separate sample is analysed.

These are the notes made after the first impression of Angus' writing has been added to the dominants, the Form Level appraisal and the first checking of the traits chart. I have explained in brackets how the notes are derived from the graphological data on the charts.

First impression. Strength and individuality of character. Some force. (Not derived from any specific examination.)

Dominants. A forward-thrusting nature (*right slant, dynamism*) which demants a wide arena for activity and fulfilment (*large dimension*). An extrovert (signs above), whose world-conquering self-projection (*near-invasive layout, small margins*) almost flouts caution but is modified by a consistently and meticulously applied brain (*degree of attention*).

Form Level. Generally good. B+. What causes our reservations? Further investigation will probably show why Angus' writing is lacking in harmony and rhythm.

After checking through the traits chart. Continually looking forward (*no left tendencies*). A thinking type (*neat, simplified form with typographic capitals, precise t-bars and close i-dots*). Combines accuracy (*signs above*) with a liking for facts and for things to make sense (*angular and vertical form*). Makes a deliberate effort to be diplomatic (*increasing word dimension countered by decreasing word dimension throughout*) — a sign of self-knowledge and growing maturity. Shows a slight tendency towards acquisitiveness or self-interest (*downward curves on s — which makes an original arc from upper right zone to lower left: the physical energy of the understrokes is also directed towards the lower left area of self-interest*). Feeling largely unconscious (*no loops, no roundness, no rogue loops — but a tiny tendency in d and t*) which means the beginning, or the phasing out, of pride and self-pity. Consistently extroverted attitude (*right slant, no left tendencies, large dimension, minimal right margins, signature invariably to the right*) but with a mind centred as much on current details as on the future (*precise t-bars, i-dots, some initial strokes, last-minute avoidance of invading on right margin, full stop after signature, vertical form, consistent organization and partial connection*). Physical energy mainly directed towards acquiring (*lower left directing of understrokes*) but a sensuous nature (*slight pastiness in all samples*). Not a robustly earthy nature (*light pressure* — masked by photocopy); energy is mainly from the psyche and the libido (*dynamism and acceleration with upper right tendencies and light pressure*). The sensuous quality is backed by the *underlining signature embellishment* which relates chiefly to the forename, showing a desire for style or histrionic expression. This could appear in a work environment once people and surroundings become familiar.

The general picture is of someone who believes the world is at his feet, waiting for him to move in, use it and organize it! Being developed in all three zones, there is no lack of balance in the personality, but the feeling function is not projected. The use of the forename in a formal signature shows a cordial manner rather than a feeling nature.

7. Re-checking the Traits Chart
Before moving on to the shaping of the final portrait, it is important to check that all data has been included and blended into the analysis.

Looking once more at the pattern of circles on Angus' trait chart we find that the following signs have not been mentioned yet:

Irregular word spacing	Occasional entanglement
Leanness	Rising baseline
Concentrated script	i-dots sometimes moving
Arcade connection	Careful punctuation
Spaced out envelope	Needle endings
Clear form	Pseudo copybook
Slight irregularity	Small capitals, especially 'I'

So the first rough sketch must be amended to include these qualities.

The clear form and pseudo-copybook letter form both show uncontrived and effortless communication, and with the rising baseline, they contribute to the extrovert picture already painted.

The small capitals show an unwillingness to exert or accept authority,but the personal 'I' may eventually become embellished (see Fig. 54).

The slight — very slight — irregularity, the moving i-dots and the occasional entanglement show imagination and fluctuating impressionability of idea. The entanglement supports the view that in this character mind dominates matter, and added to the many other powerful traits in this writing may imply the degree of obsession with an idea necessary for achieving distinction.

We should note at this point that the striking appearance of Angus' writing does not lie in the letter form, which is pseudo-copybook and without a great deal of originality, but in its dynamism, dimension, rightward slant and general extrovert movement.

The concentration of the letter of application (see Fig. 124) is circumstantial and is not found in the other samples except for the point at the end of Fig. 125 where he is running out of space. (Note that even there the signature is enlarged, complete and embellished, showing a dislike of being curbed or cramped.) The envelope, whose address is well to the right, shows Angus' need for space, for a large arena for activity. We can accept a small degree of intense and immediate involvement (concentrated script) if Angus tells us that he tends to write this way during examinations of any kind.

We come now to a small group of traits whose properties were almost submerged by the powerful drives of forward-seeking and accuracy. Leanness, arcade connection, needle endings and irregular word spacing all relate to social behaviour, and, in the light of a complete absence of roundness or looping, indicate coldness in relationships.

Leanness — prudence, caution and withholding. The head rules the heart, particularly when accompanied by a need for facts, reasons and concrete realization.

Arcade connection — a screening of the feelings: a proud, lofty or snobbish approach. In the context of this writing the standard of forward-moving and accuracy will make it difficult for the writer to suffer fools gladly, or to pity lack of success.

Needle endings — the will is made manifestly clear, and in this case we know that the will drives forward. Brakes — caution and accuracy — are applied for logical, not feeling reasons. There is a certain ruthlessness in this projection of will.

Irregular word spacing — a confusingly unpredictable need of people. One minute the writer wants company, the next — down come the shutters. Even if the motive for this type of social behaviour is not selfish, it appears so and it can be hurtful.

We can now see why the Form Level and harmony suffer a small reduction: this powerful character conveys no impression of immediate warmth or compassion. However, the regularity of the writing in all samples shows constancy, and he is likely to be loyal to those with whom he has established a good mental relationship.

8. The Full Analysis

How are we going to arrange our wealth of information into a clear portrait? Do we need to write a lucid essay? Many graphologists no longer believe that this is necessary, and that a blending of qualities actually confuses. As long as all tendencies and traits are fairly contrasted, compared and grouped, the final portrait need not be a literary one.

Nevertheless, the information will have to be presented in a system of some kind. It is true that any isolated comment is of great interest to the writer, and this explains why the interpretation of dominants alone is always popular, and why learner graphologists do actually feel some measure of success as they try to master this complex study! But we cannot offer an analysis as a completed work if it does not have unity and shape.

The subtitles which follow, carefully and correctly illustrated with data, can represent a full analysis, and can be used by graphologists in the knowledge that they cover the spectrum of qualities normally assessed. Graphologists who decide to specialize in such areas as crime, sexual deviation or personnel selection devise relevant categories after profound research and we shall not be advancing to these.

(a)   Short description of the writer's nature.

(b) His manner — which may be quite different.
(c) What he wants out of life.
(d) What he puts in. (Gifts.)
(e) Educational standard.
(f) Social tendencies and behaviour.
(g) Psychologically different areas.
(h) A therapeutic environment for the writer.

We can now move on to the analysis.

Name: Angus Piper

The nature of the writer
A confident person, who, if self-doubt ever arises, shrugs it away and moves on into the future. Ambition and optimism come naturally to him, as do the faculties of attentiveness and accuracy. The mental, physical and idealistic areas of his nature are all well-developed, but need space and scope for fulfilment. This individual could become mentally aggressive if cramped or forced to limit his horizons, but his self-discipline is considerable.

His manner
Frequently flamboyant, but less so in formal situations. His sense of confidence may be overpowering and he may appear snobbish or arrogant. He will generally appear outgoing and ready to welcome new experiences. Any unguarded or unfortunate comment will immediately be corrected, since caution and diplomacy (at present tested severely by his forward-thrusting energy) modify his actions. This sign of growing maturity may soon extend to other areas of behaviour.

What he wants out of life
There is a desire for material comfort and possessions, but the urge to excel is only partly connected with it. His real wish is to exploit his own capabilities to the full, and he knows and understands these well. Additionally, he wants to be seen to succeed: the appearances of trappings of success are likely to be displayed and treasured. Physical pleasures and mental or imaginative stimulation are essential to his well-being, as are opportunities for new experiences.

What he puts in
In short, a very great deal. Any work undertaken is likely to be carefully and efficiently completed, with an imaginative and dynamic approach.

Given a sufficiently attractive project, he will contribute all the painstaking energy of his nature, and is capable of forgetting his own physical needs or desires in its perfection. However, if a task or a social situation incurs his scorn, he may allow the demands of his sensuous nature and his need of mental stimulation to deflect him from participating in it at all. His powerful psychic energy requires a project which absorbs and fulfils his dynamism.

Educational standard
Ignoring the information in the job application letter, the writer clearly has penetrating mental application, accuracy and graphic ease. He absorbs and communicates knowledge easily. His thinking processes are precise yet flexible, and he prefers to come to sound and reasonable conclusions than to dwell in the abstract (though this faculty is capable of development). His certainty that his conclusions are right is less likely to lead to mistakes than to intellectual isolation, though he is quite capable of altering his conclusions if the ideas or the reasons of others are sufficiently stimulating or persuasive.

Social tendencies and behaviour
A superficial bonhomie and liking for stimulating gatherings masks a self-sufficient and unemotional nature which is inclined to be fastidious and generally cool, though loyal to established attachments. Gregarious and flamboyant at times, he will not form strong friendships easily, and may withdraw if bored, or if a more stimulating demand is made on his mind or senses. In order to accept authority he must first respect its logic and credibility. There are no signs of dishonesty.

Psychologically difficult areas
At present there are no problems, but minute signs of unconscious and therefore unresolved difficulty with feeling can be detected. This seems likely to be treated with self-imposed discipline for some time to come, shrugged away with any other unreasonable or unstimulating intrusion. The self as expressed in the personal I is in transition, and if further embellishments develop — ꐦ or ꐦ or Z— it is possible that a narcissistic preoccupation may stand between the writer and his close personal relationships — which will tend to be based on mental stimulation and sensuous response. However, a fulfilling life task should prevent this subtle and by no means established tendency from developing.

A therapeutic environment for the writer
The word means healing, and suggests that if the right environment

is adopted the character is enabled to grow positively and fulfil the
potentiality of its own nature. In Angus' case boredom and repression
must be avoided: he needs to live and work in a situation where new
doors can constantly be opened. Humdrum activity will bring out the less
attractive side of his nature, and although he has no particular urge for
dominance or authority, his need for self-assertion may appear in that
guise if his spirits and energy are cramped. Hard physical work is not for
him, nor does he need regular contact with practical or earthy processes,
though these may attract him and satisfy his sensuous nature.

9. Specialized Analysis

Many graphologists specialize in particular fields of analysis, and their
highly researched work means that they are and should be approached if
specialized knowledge — managerial skills or depth psychology are two
examples — is needed. However, many amateur graphologists are asked
for brief or informal appraisals, and we can treat Angus' letter of
application in that way.

Non-specialist personal selection
We should omit the first two (a and b) and the last two (g and h)
categories of full analysis, picking relevant points from them if we believe
those comments to be helpful. Thus:

The writer knows and understands his own capabilities, and wishes to
exploit these capabilities to the full. It is important to him to succeed and
also to be seen to be successful. In short, he is ambitious.

Any work undertaken is likely to be carefully and efficiently completed,
with an imaginative and dynamic approach. Given a sufficiently
attractive project, he will contribute all the painstaking energy of his
nature, and is capable of forgetting his own physical needs or desires in
its perfection. However, if a task (or social situation) incurs his scorn, he
may allow the demands of his sensuous nature and his need of mental
stimulation to deflect him from participating in it at all. His powerful
psychic energy requires a project which absorbs and fulfils its dynamism.

Apart from the given educational successes, the writer clearly has
penetrating mental application, accuracy and graphic ease. He absorbs
and communicates knowledge easily. His thinking processes are precise
yet flexible, and he prefers to come to sound and reasonable conclusions
than to dwell in the abstract, though this faculty is capable of
development. His certainty that his conclusions are right is less likely to
lead to mistakes than to intellectual isolation, though he is quite capable
of altering his conclusions if the ideas or the reasons of others are

sufficiently stimulating or persuasive.

His social manner is likely to be extrovert and enthusiastic and — when people and surroundings become familiar — may be flamboyant at times. But this bonhomie and liking for stimulating gatherings is largely superficial, and masks a self-sufficient and unemotional nature which is inclined to be fastidious and generally cool. He will not form strong friendships easily, and may withdraw socially if bored, or if a more stimulating demand is made on his mind or senses. However, he is loyal to established attachments. In order to accept authority he must first respect its logic and credibility. There are no signs of dishonesty.

The writer is best suited to work which involves thinking, but needs opportunities for innovation and change of routine.

This brief report illustrates several important aspects of making an analysis. Firstly, it can be seen that an essay portrait is made simply by removing the subtitles and creating a new opening sentence. Secondly, the graphologist's opinion of the writer's suitability for a job, marriage or custodial detention is not required: those who have asked for the report know what they are looking for and will seek for it in the data you provide.

Thirdly, there is no point in offering irrelevant information. Deeply personal matters affect the writing temporarily without forming an integral part of the writer's nature, and outsiders do not need to know about them unless they are going to influence the role under discussion.

Incidentally, Angus did not submit the job application. Since he was beginning a university course in October, he was looking for temporary employment only, and eventually decided to spend six months in Australia instead.

10. Becoming a Graphologist

Almost anyone can learn the information in this workbook and gain practical experience in eye training. With more effort, they can become proficient in sifting and comparing data for a full analysis.

It is improbable that anyone new to the subject could absorb the contents of this workbook in less than two years, which is a relatively short study course. Remembering St Augustine's caution that 'nothing excellent was ever wrought suddenly', and limiting learning to one aspect at a time, will train your eyes. But sharing the movements of a lone individual as he enters and crosses the white page of world space rquires a deeper sense of compassion and involvement, and that is where the practice of graphology begins.

Index